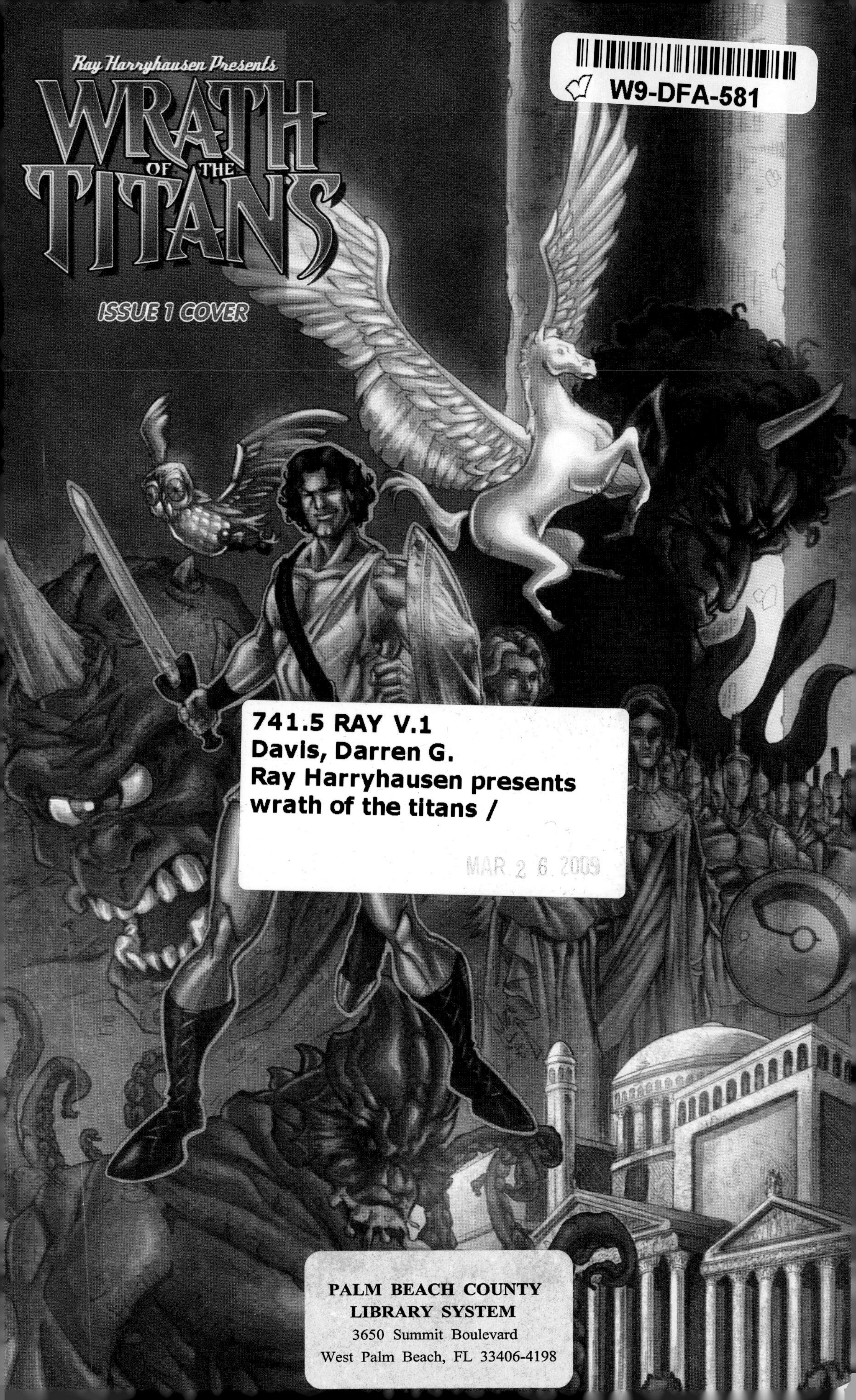
Ray Harryhausen Presents
WRATH OF THE TITANS
ISSUE 1 COVER

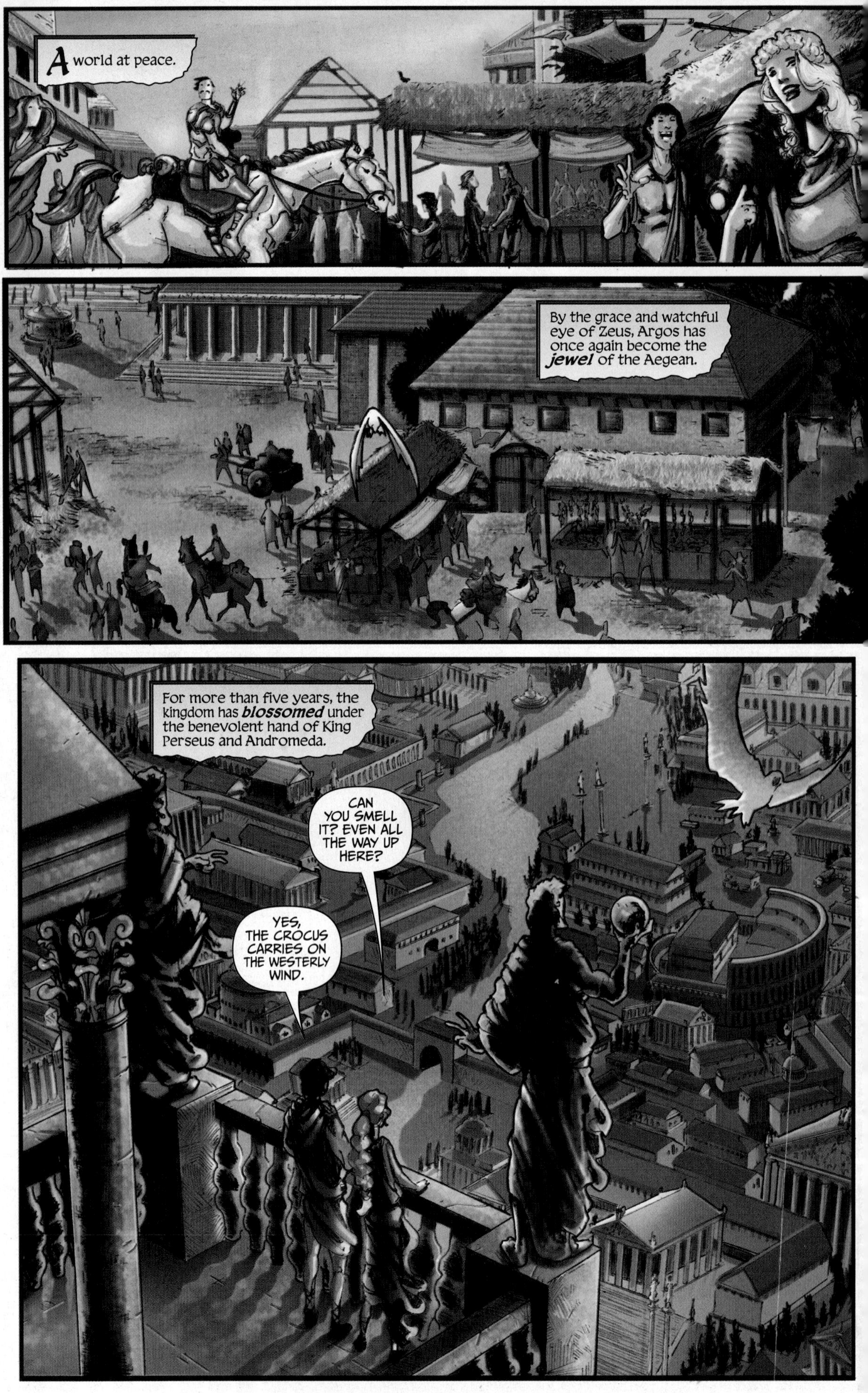
A world at peace.
By the grace and watchful eye of Zeus, Argos has once again become the *jewel* of the Aegean.
For more than five years, the kingdom has *blossomed* under the benevolent hand of King Perseus and Andromeda.
CAN YOU SMELL IT? EVEN ALL THE WAY UP HERE?
YES, THE CROCUS CARRIES ON THE WESTERLY WIND.

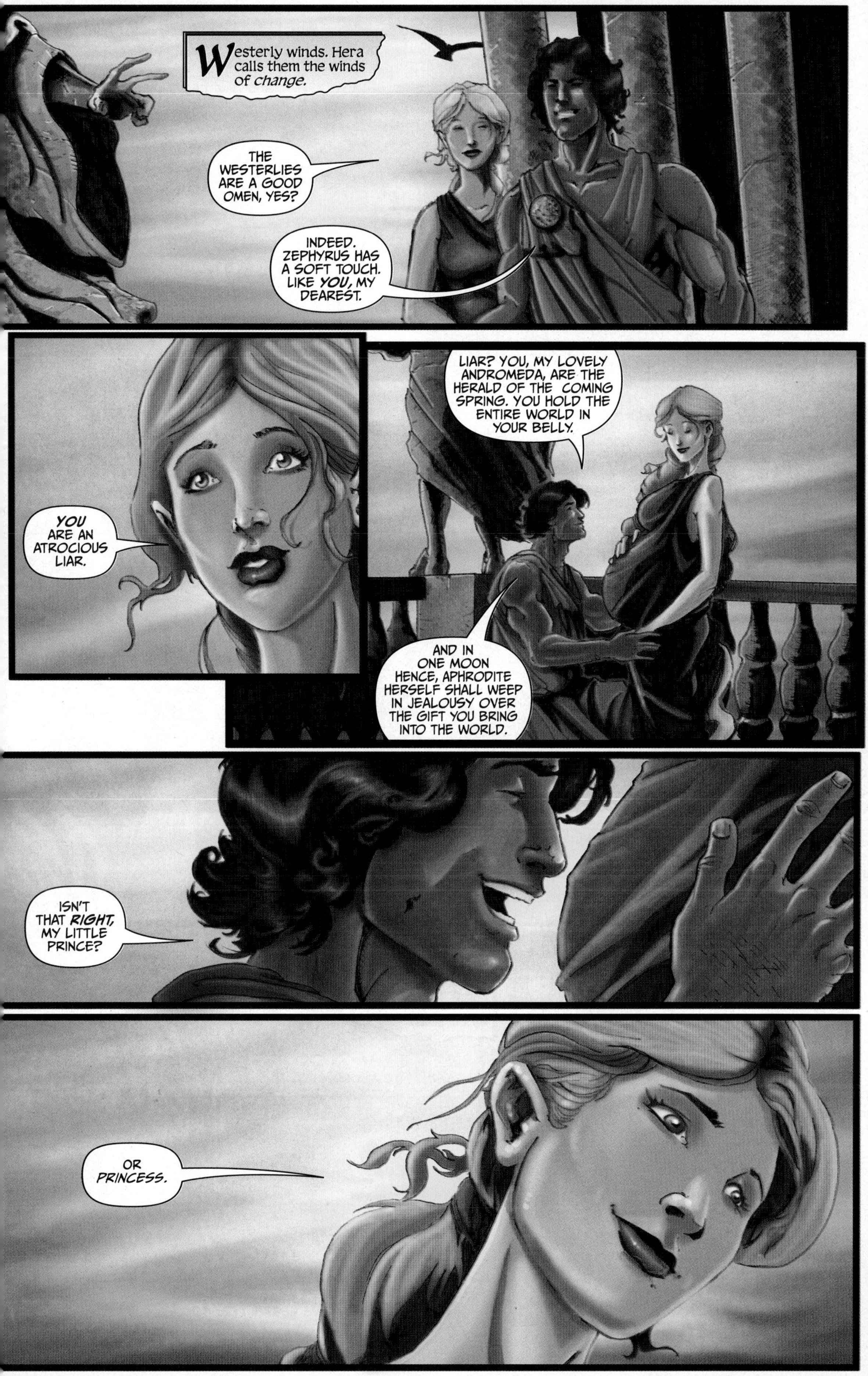
Westerly winds. Hera calls them the winds of *change.*
THE WESTERLIES ARE A GOOD OMEN, YES?
INDEED. ZEPHYRUS HAS A SOFT TOUCH. LIKE *YOU*, MY DEAREST.
YOU ARE AN ATROCIOUS LIAR.
LIAR? YOU, MY LOVELY ANDROMEDA, ARE THE HERALD OF THE COMING SPRING. YOU HOLD THE ENTIRE WORLD IN YOUR BELLY.
AND IN ONE MOON HENCE, APHRODITE HERSELF SHALL WEEP IN JEALOUSY OVER THE GIFT YOU BRING INTO THE WORLD.
ISN'T THAT *RIGHT*, MY LITTLE PRINCE?
OR *PRINCESS.*

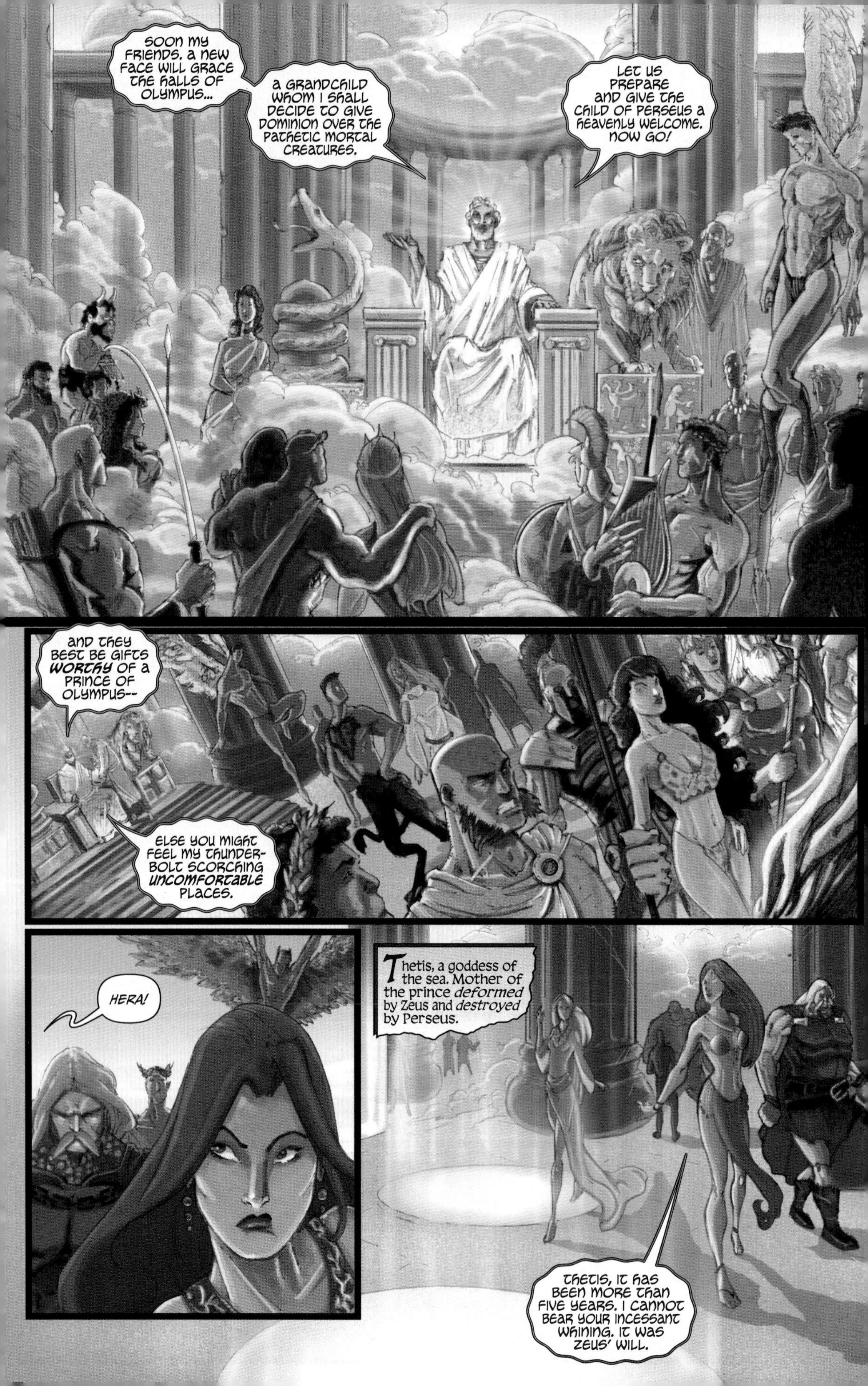
SOON MY FRIENDS, A NEW FACE WILL GRACE THE HALLS OF OLYMPUS...
A GRANDCHILD WHOM I SHALL DECIDE TO GIVE DOMINION OVER THE PATHETIC MORTAL CREATURES.
LET US PREPARE AND GIVE THE CHILD OF PERSEUS A HEAVENLY WELCOME. NOW GO!
AND THEY BEST BE GIFTS WORTHY OF A PRINCE OF OLYMPUS--
ELSE YOU MIGHT FEEL MY THUNDER-BOLT SCORCHING UNCOMFORTABLE PLACES.
HERA!
Thetis, a goddess of the sea. Mother of the prince deformed by Zeus and destroyed by Perseus.
THETIS, IT HAS BEEN MORE THAN FIVE YEARS. I CANNOT BEAR YOUR INCESSANT WHINING. IT WAS ZEUS' WILL.

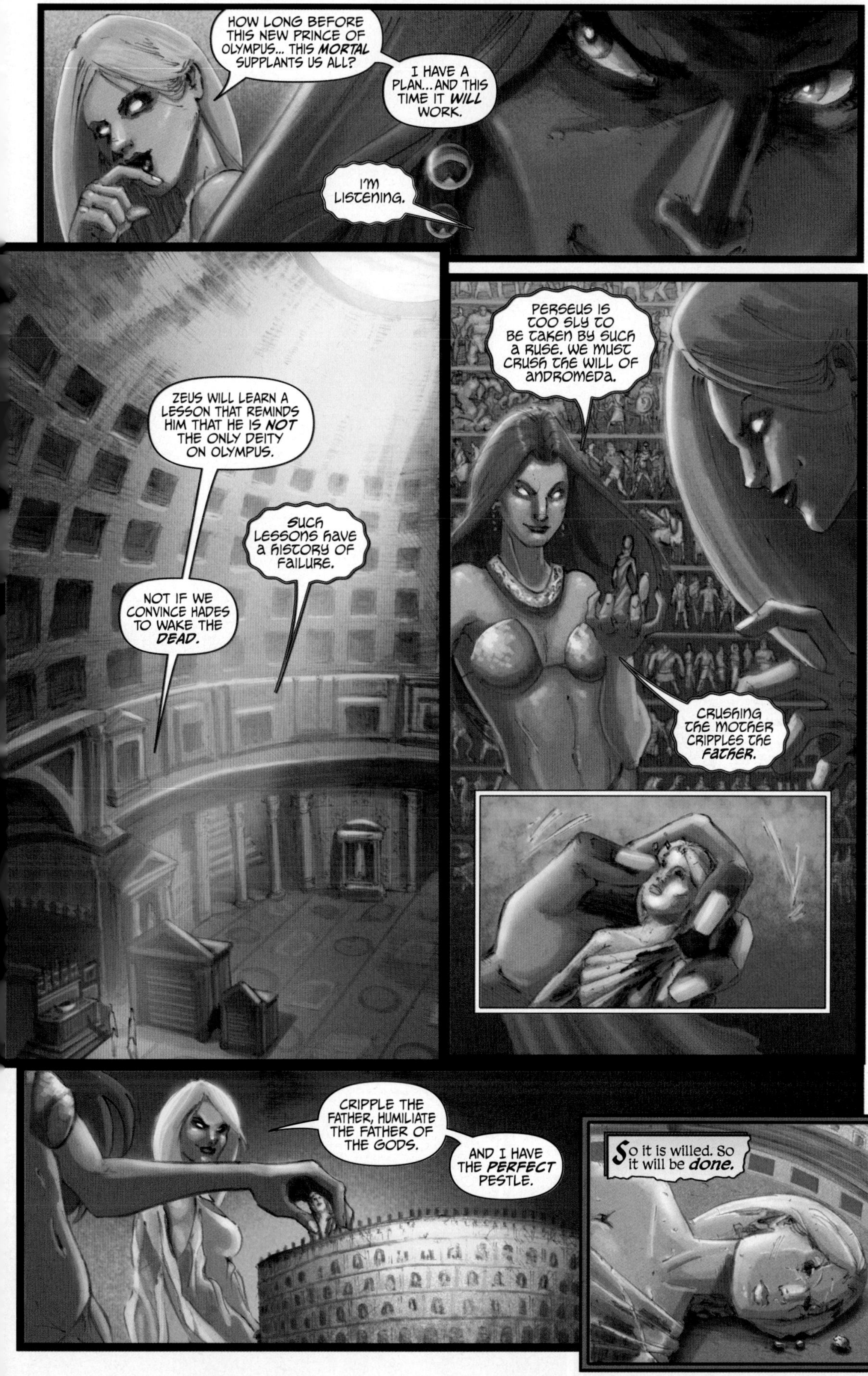
HOW LONG BEFORE THIS NEW PRINCE OF OLYMPUS... THIS MORTAL SUPPLANTS US ALL?
I HAVE A PLAN... AND THIS TIME IT WILL WORK.
I'M LISTENING.
ZEUS WILL LEARN A LESSON THAT REMINDS HIM THAT HE IS NOT THE ONLY DEITY ON OLYMPUS.
SUCH LESSONS HAVE A HISTORY OF FAILURE.
NOT IF WE CONVINCE HADES TO WAKE THE DEAD.
PERSEUS IS TOO SLY TO BE TAKEN BY SUCH A RUSE. WE MUST CRUSH THE WILL OF ANDROMEDA.
CRUSHING THE MOTHER CRIPPLES THE FATHER.
CRIPPLE THE FATHER, HUMILIATE THE FATHER OF THE GODS.
AND I HAVE THE PERFECT PESTLE.
So it is willed. So it will be done.

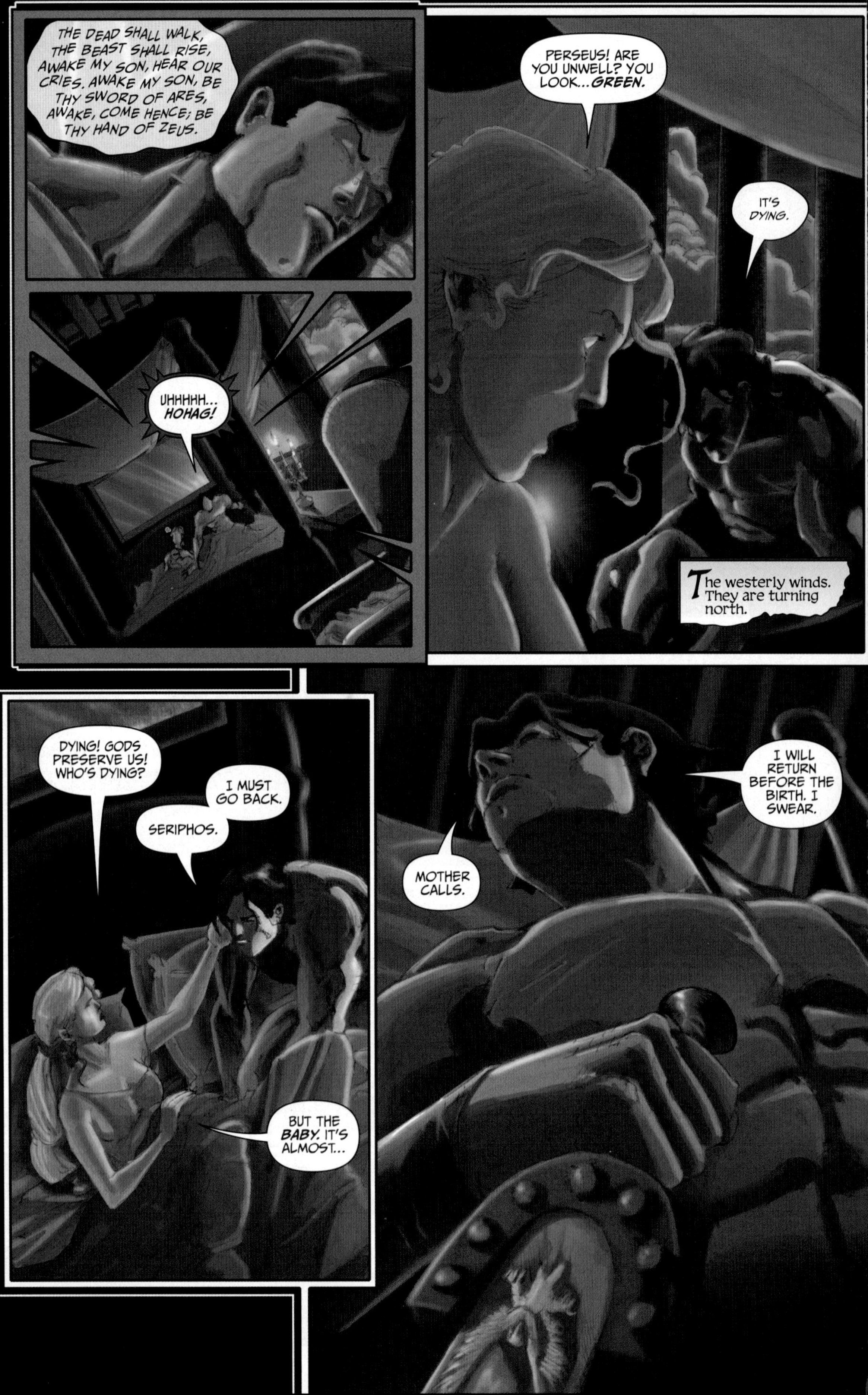
THE DEAD SHALL WALK, THE BEAST SHALL RISE, AWAKE MY SON, HEAR OUR CRIES. AWAKE MY SON, BE THY SWORD OF ARES, AWAKE, COME HENCE; BE THY HAND OF ZEUS.
UHHHHH... HOHAG!
PERSEUS! ARE YOU UNWELL? YOU LOOK... GREEN.
IT'S DYING.
The westerly winds. They are turning north.
DYING! GODS PRESERVE US! WHO'S DYING?
I MUST GO BACK.
SERIPHOS.
BUT THE BABY. IT'S ALMOST...
MOTHER CALLS.
I WILL RETURN BEFORE THE BIRTH. I SWEAR.

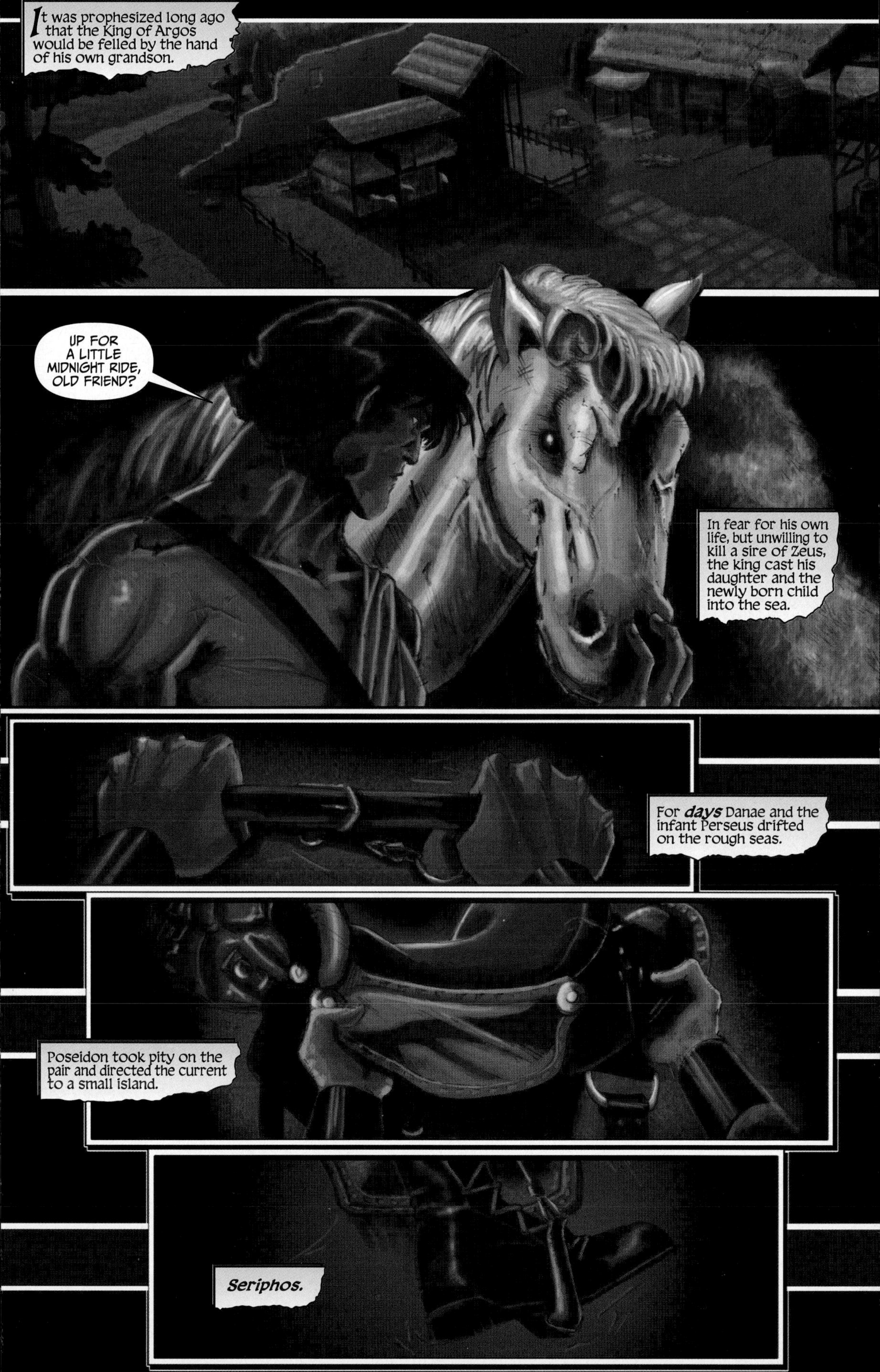
It was prophesized long ago that the King of Argos would be felled by the hand of his own grandson.
UP FOR A LITTLE MIDNIGHT RIDE, OLD FRIEND?
In fear for his own life, but unwilling to kill a sire of Zeus, the king cast his daughter and the newly born child into the sea.
For *days* Danae and the infant Perseus drifted on the rough seas.
Poseidon took pity on the pair and directed the current to a small island.
Seriphos.

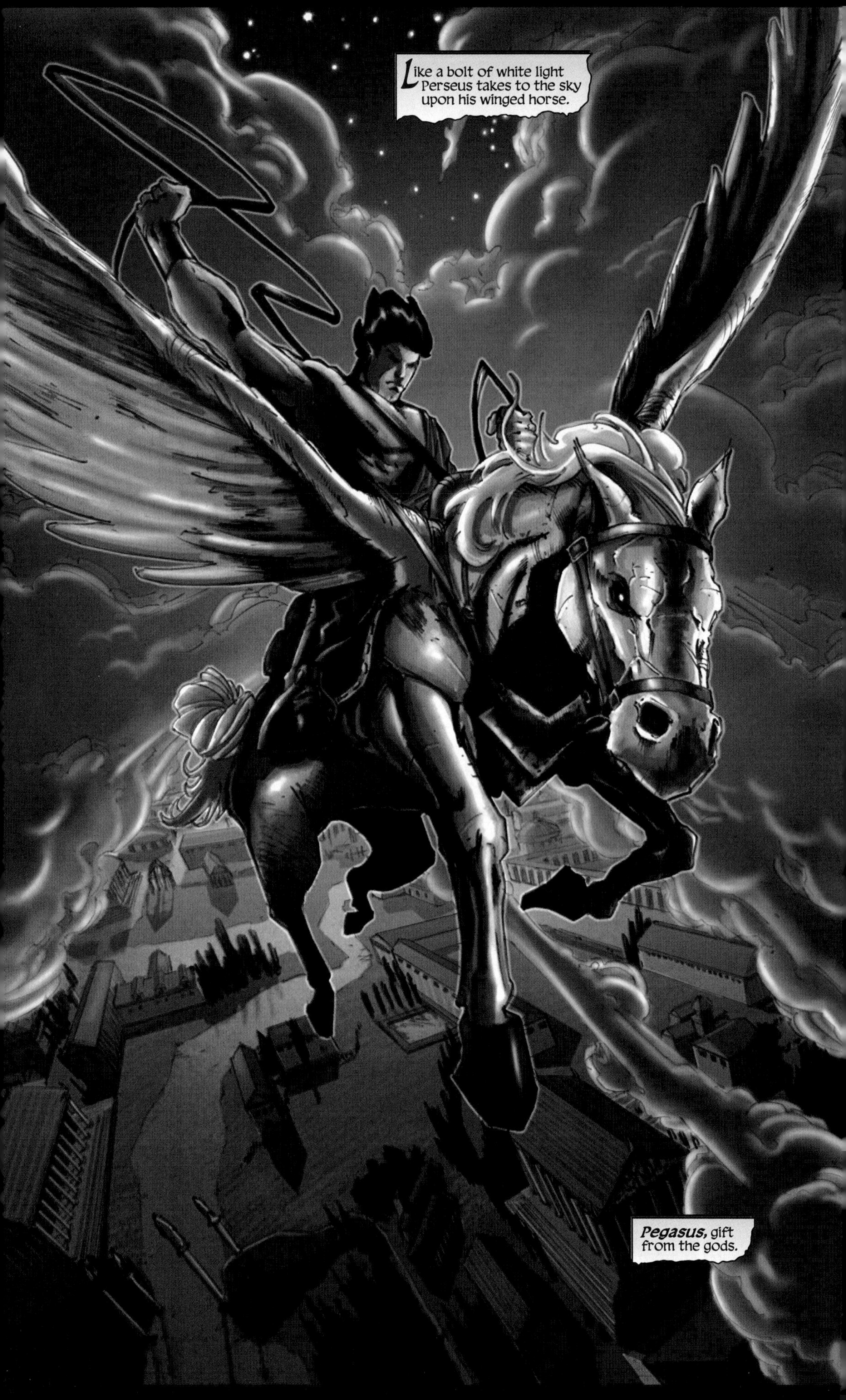
Like a bolt of white light Perseus takes to the sky upon his winged horse.
Pegasus, gift from the gods.

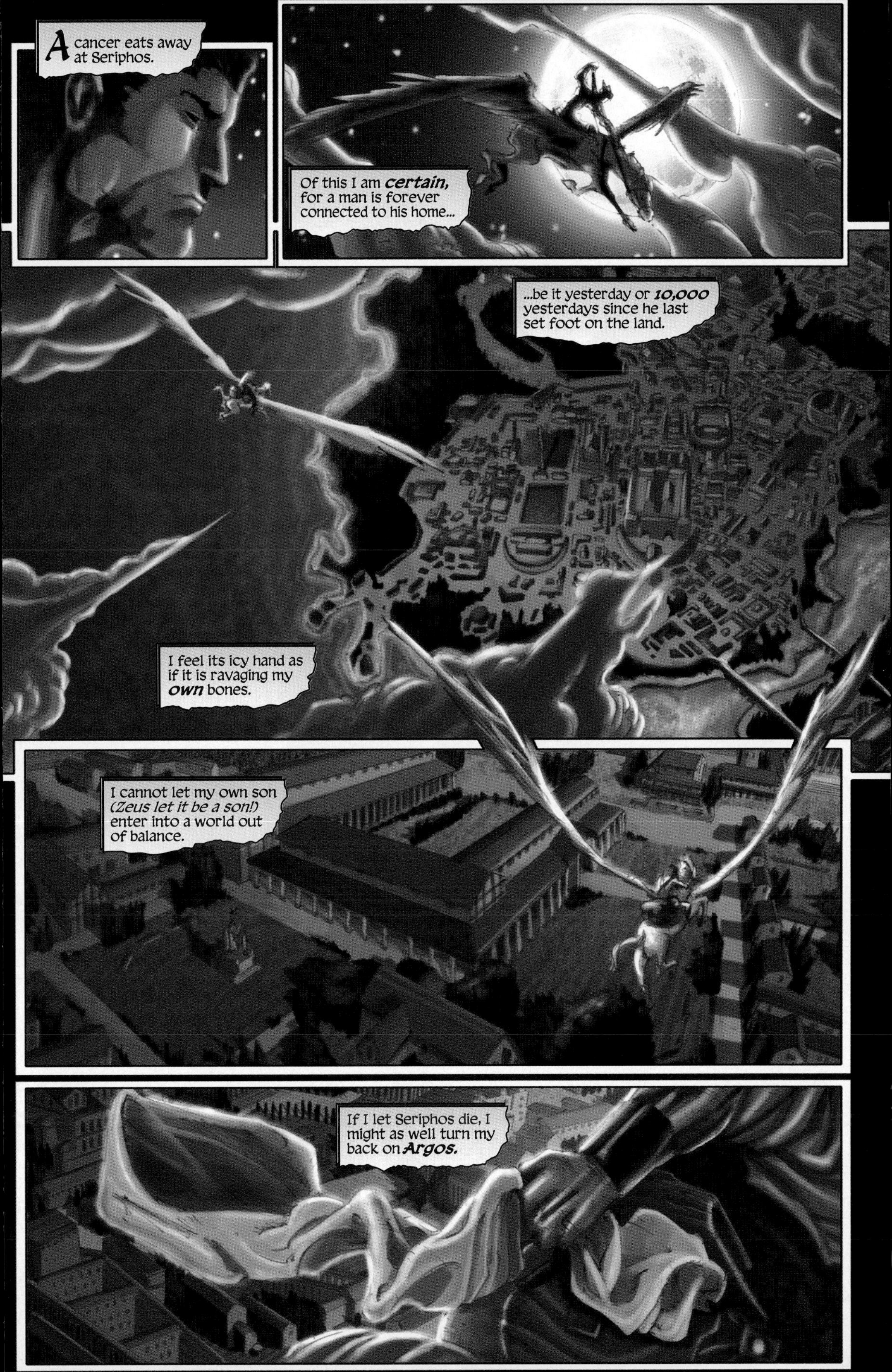
A cancer eats away at Seriphos.
Of this I am *certain,* for a man is forever connected to his home...
...be it yesterday or *10,000* yesterdays since he last set foot on the land.
I feel its icy hand as if it is ravaging my *own* bones.
I cannot let my own son *(Zeus let it be a son!)* enter into a world out of balance.
If I let Seriphos die, I might as well turn my back on *Argos.*

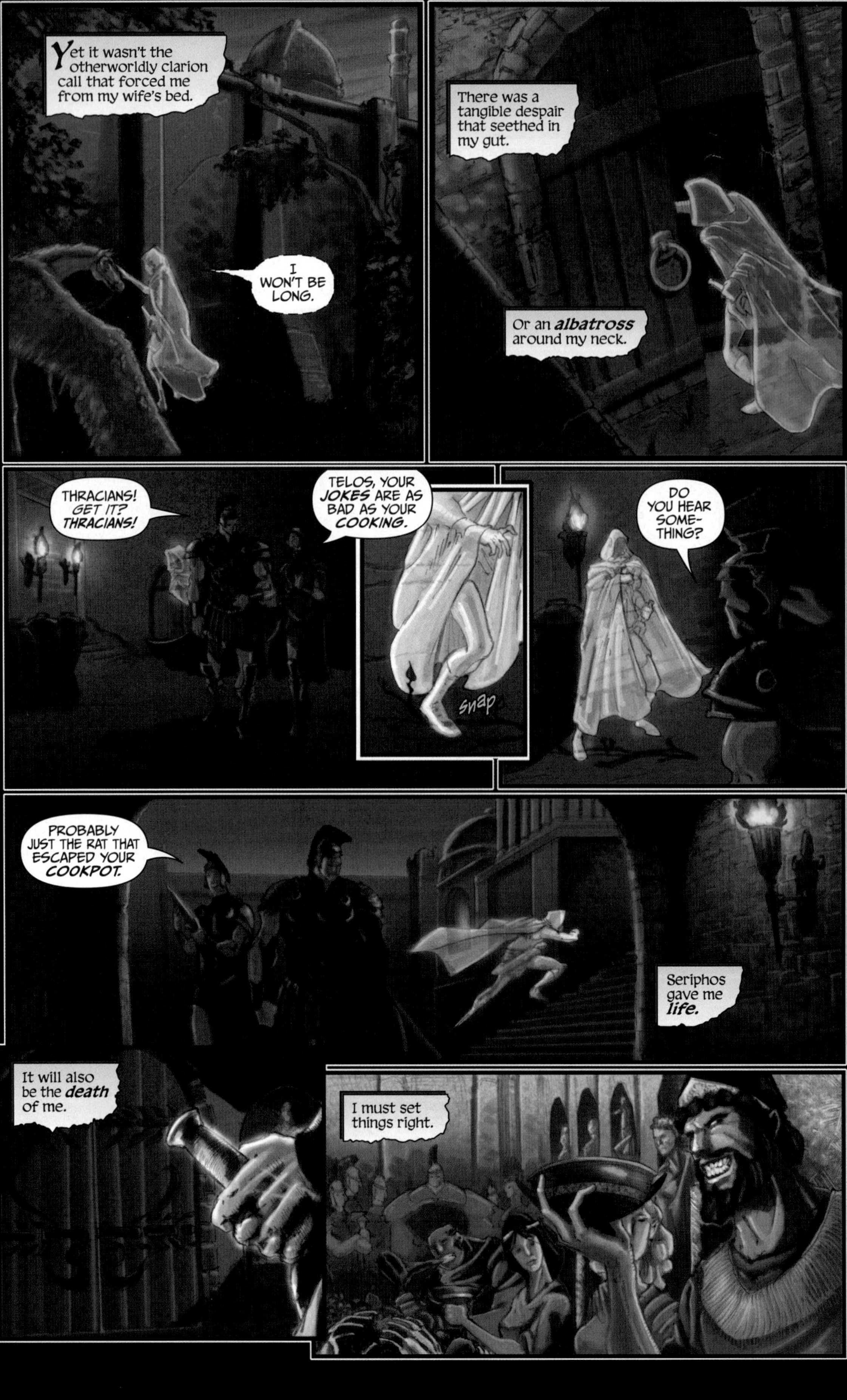

Yet it wasn't the otherworldly clarion call that forced me from my wife's bed.
I WON'T BE LONG.
There was a tangible despair that seethed in my gut.
Or an albatross around my neck.
THRACIANS! GET IT? THRACIANS!
TELOS, YOUR JOKES ARE AS BAD AS YOUR COOKING.
SNAP
DO YOU HEAR SOME-THING?
PROBABLY JUST THE RAT THAT ESCAPED YOUR COOKPOT.
Seriphos gave me life.
It will also be the death of me.
I must set things right.

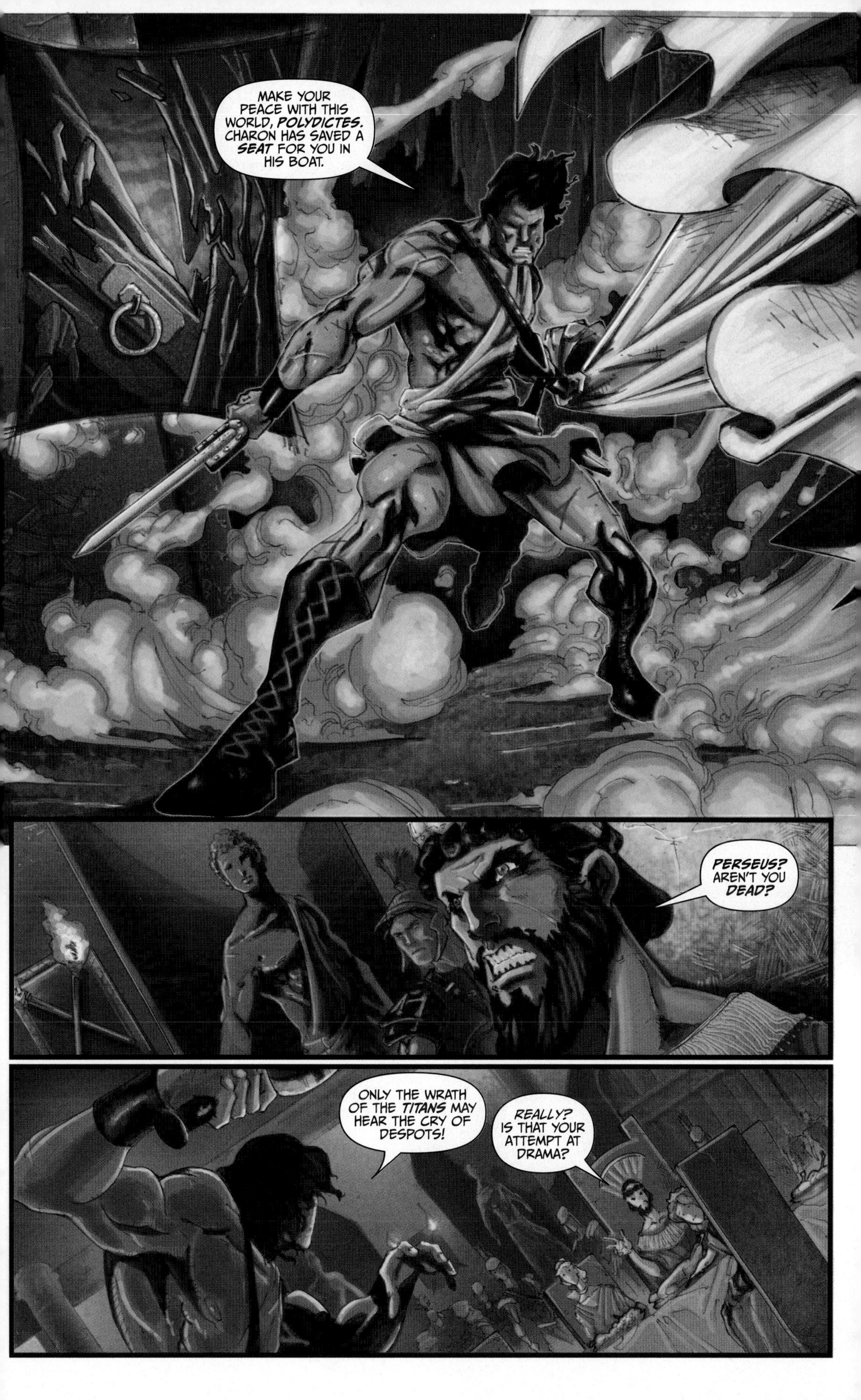
MAKE YOUR PEACE WITH THIS WORLD, *POLYDICTES.* CHARON HAS SAVED A *SEAT* FOR YOU IN HIS BOAT.
PERSEUS? AREN'T YOU *DEAD?*
ONLY THE WRATH OF THE *TITANS* MAY HEAR THE CRY OF DESPOTS!
REALLY? IS THAT YOUR ATTEMPT AT DRAMA?

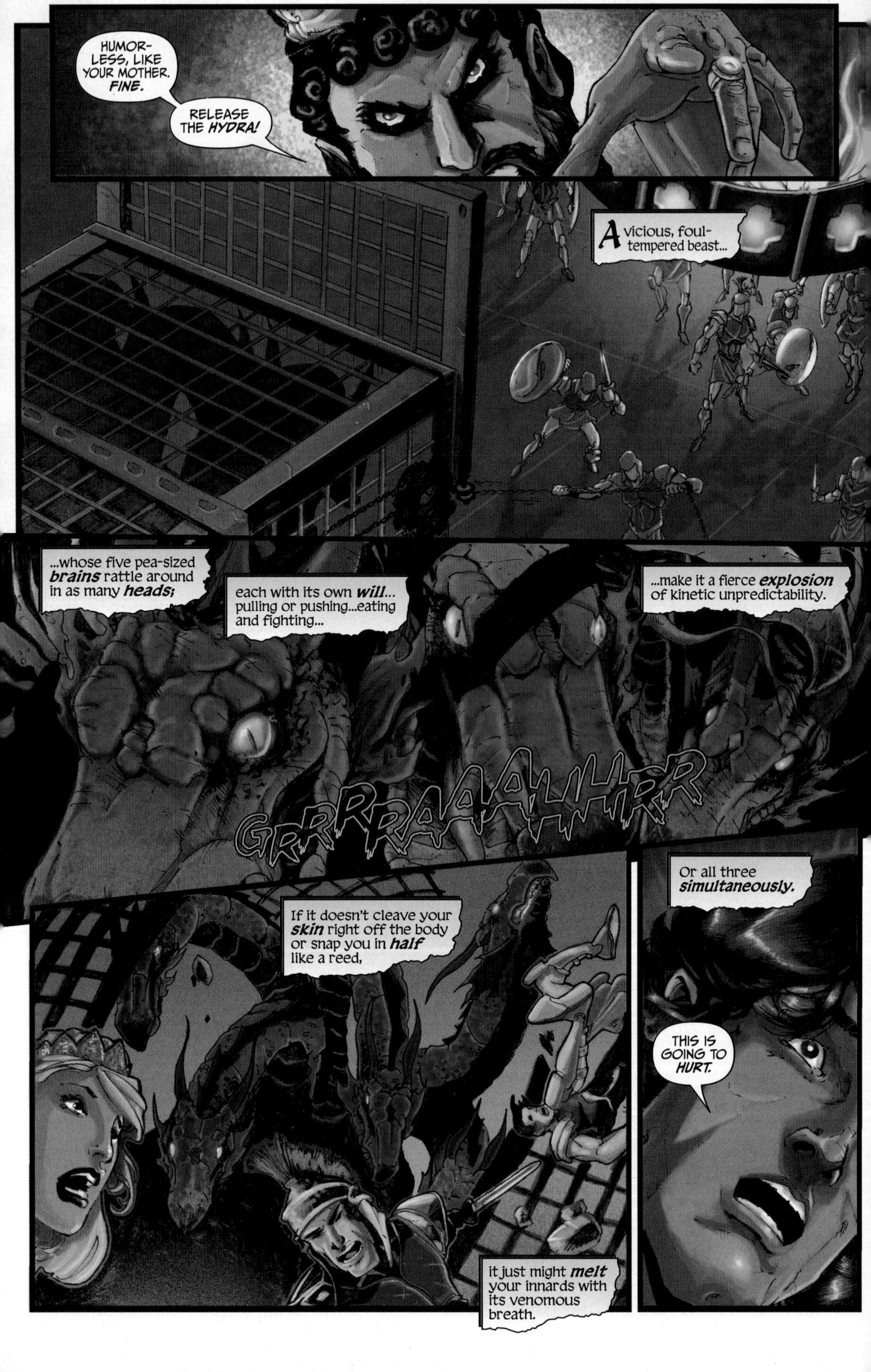

HUMORLESS, LIKE YOUR MOTHER. FINE.
RELEASE THE HYDRA!
A vicious, foul-tempered beast...
...whose five pea-sized brains rattle around in as many heads;
each with its own will... pulling or pushing...eating and fighting...
...make it a fierce explosion of kinetic unpredictability.
GRRRRAAAAHHRR
If it doesn't cleave your skin right off the body or snap you in half like a reed,
it just might melt your innards with its venomous breath.
Or all three simultaneously.
THIS IS GOING TO HURT.

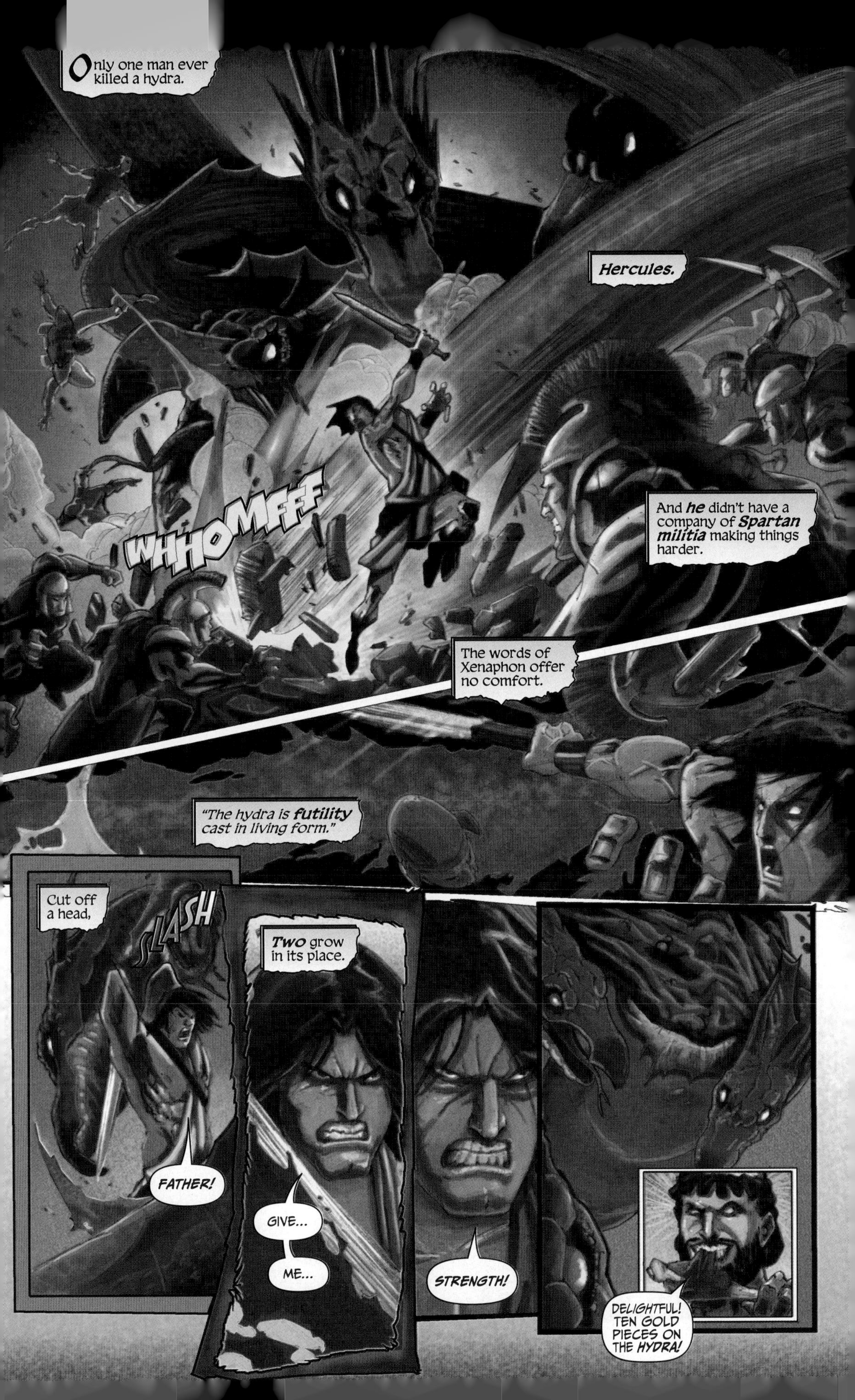
Only one man ever killed a hydra.
Hercules.
WHHOMFFF
And he didn't have a company of Spartan militia making things harder.
The words of Xenaphon offer no comfort.
"The hydra is futility cast in living form."
Cut off a head,
SLASH
FATHER!
Two grow in its place.
GIVE...
ME...
STRENGTH!
DELIGHTFUL! TEN GOLD PIECES ON THE HYDRA!

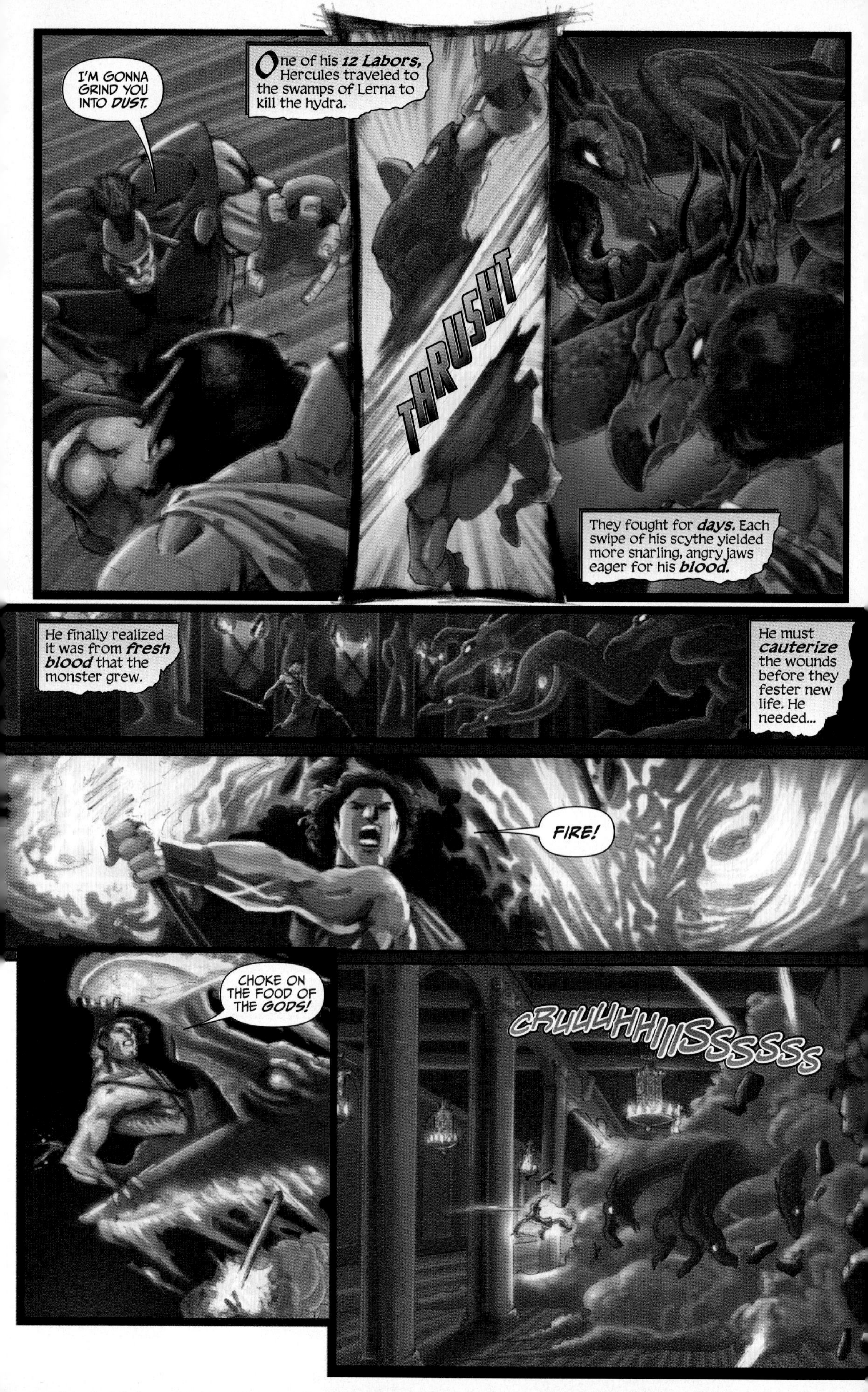
I'M GONNA GRIND YOU INTO DUST.
One of his 12 Labors, Hercules traveled to the swamps of Lerna to kill the hydra.
THRUSHT
They fought for days. Each swipe of his scythe yielded more snarling, angry jaws eager for his blood.
He finally realized it was from fresh blood that the monster grew.
He must cauterize the wounds before they fester new life. He needed...
FIRE!
CHOKE ON THE FOOD OF THE GODS!
CRUUUHHIIISSSSSS

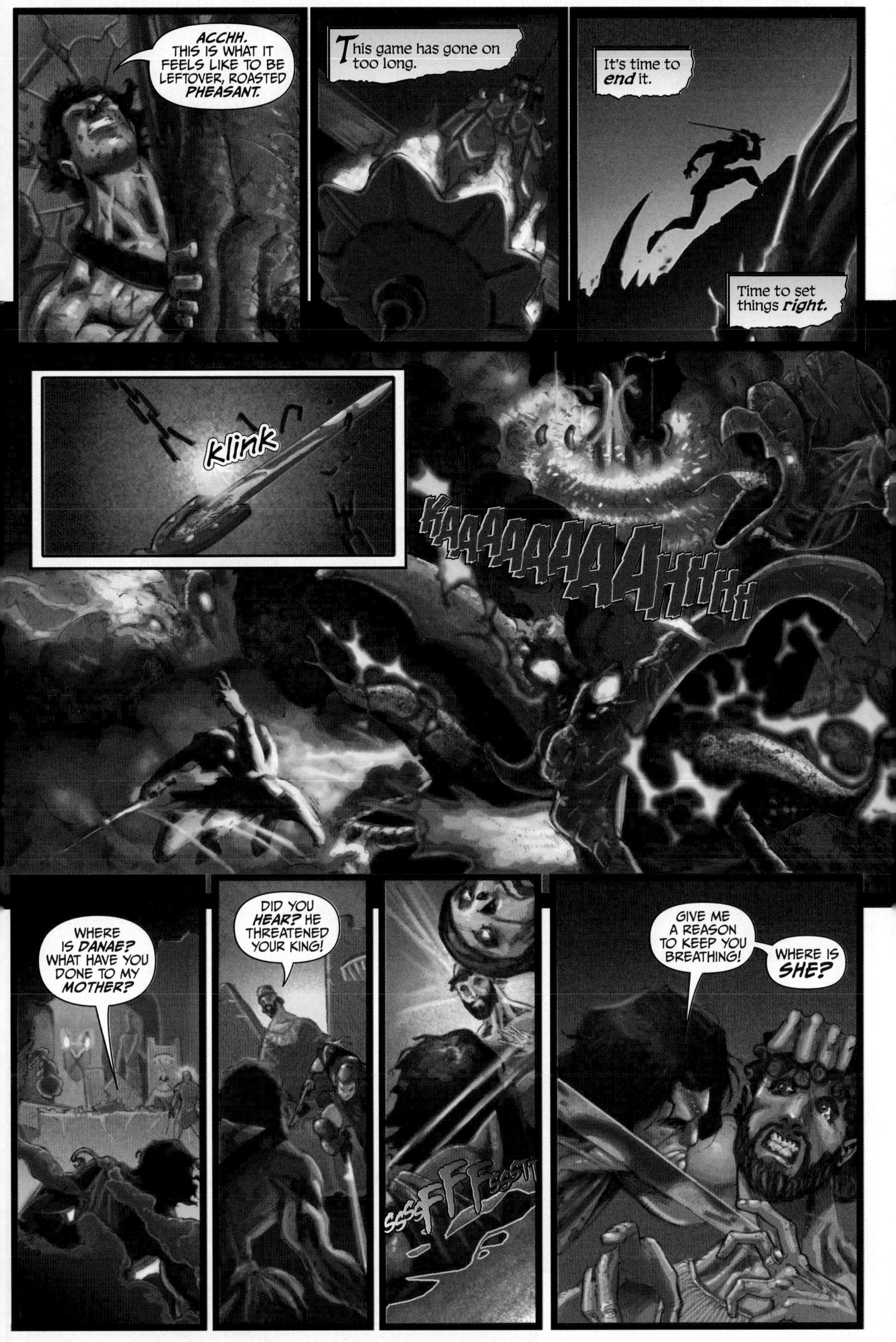
ACCHH. THIS IS WHAT IT FEELS LIKE TO BE LEFTOVER, ROASTED PHEASANT.
This game has gone on too long.
It's time to end it.
Time to set things right.
klink
KAAAAAAAAHHHH
WHERE IS DANAE? WHAT HAVE YOU DONE TO MY MOTHER?
DID YOU HEAR? HE THREATENED YOUR KING!
SSSSFFFSSSTT
GIVE ME A REASON TO KEEP YOU BREATHING!
WHERE IS SHE?

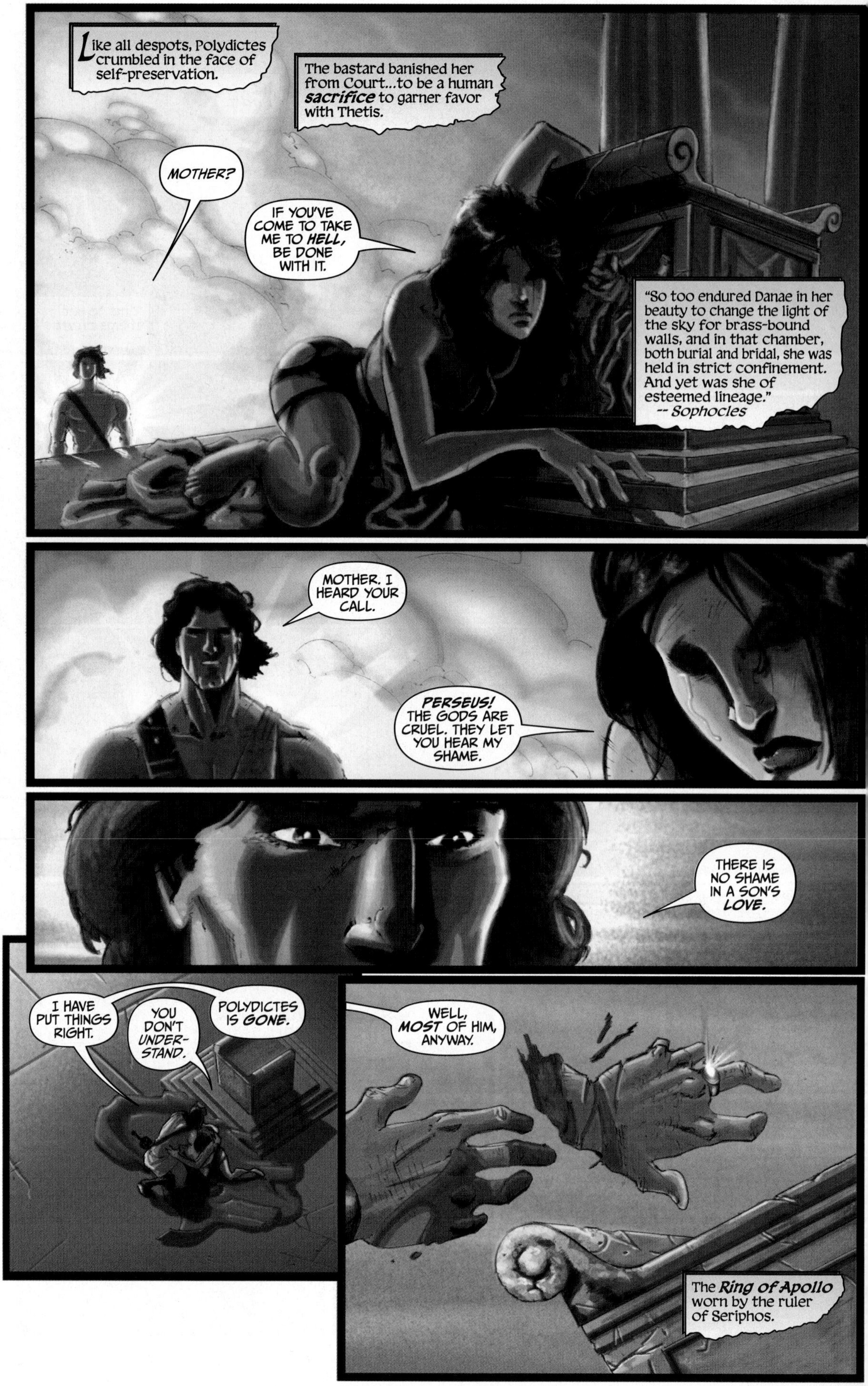
Like all despots, Polydictes crumbled in the face of self-preservation.
The bastard banished her from Court...to be a human sacrifice to garner favor with Thetis.
MOTHER?
IF YOU'VE COME TO TAKE ME TO HELL, BE DONE WITH IT.
"So too endured Danae in her beauty to change the light of the sky for brass-bound walls, and in that chamber, both burial and bridal, she was held in strict confinement. And yet was she of esteemed lineage."
-- Sophocles
MOTHER. I HEARD YOUR CALL.
PERSEUS! THE GODS ARE CRUEL. THEY LET YOU HEAR MY SHAME.
THERE IS NO SHAME IN A SON'S LOVE.
I HAVE PUT THINGS RIGHT.
YOU DON'T UNDER-STAND.
POLYDICTES IS GONE.
WELL, MOST OF HIM, ANYWAY.
The Ring of Apollo worn by the ruler of Seriphos.

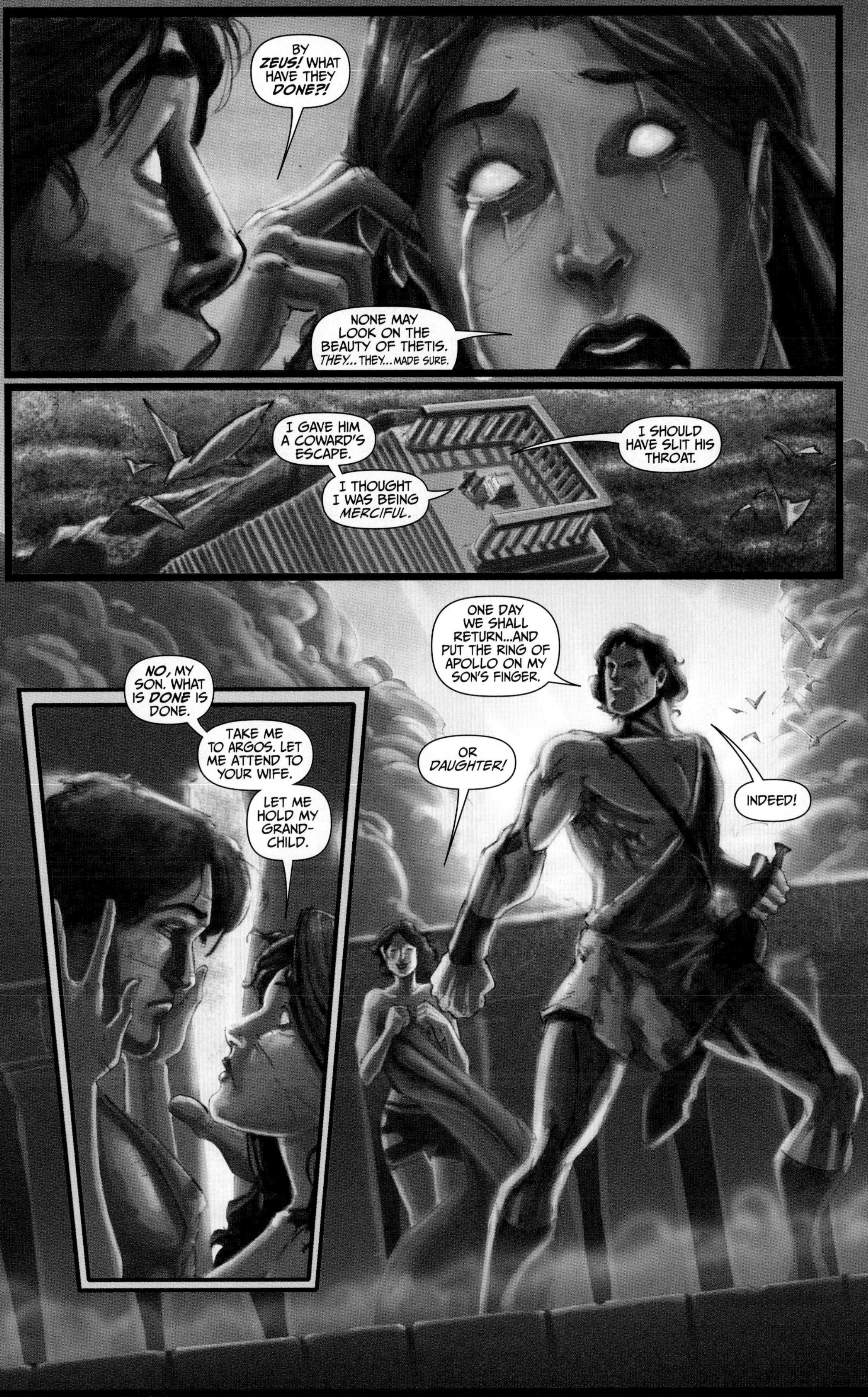
BY ZEUS! WHAT HAVE THEY DONE?!
NONE MAY LOOK ON THE BEAUTY OF THETIS. THEY... THEY... MADE SURE.
I GAVE HIM A COWARD'S ESCAPE.
I THOUGHT I WAS BEING MERCIFUL.
I SHOULD HAVE SLIT HIS THROAT.
NO, MY SON. WHAT IS DONE IS DONE.
TAKE ME TO ARGOS. LET ME ATTEND TO YOUR WIFE.
LET ME HOLD MY GRAND-CHILD.
ONE DAY WE SHALL RETURN...AND PUT THE RING OF APOLLO ON MY SON'S FINGER.
OR DAUGHTER!
INDEED!

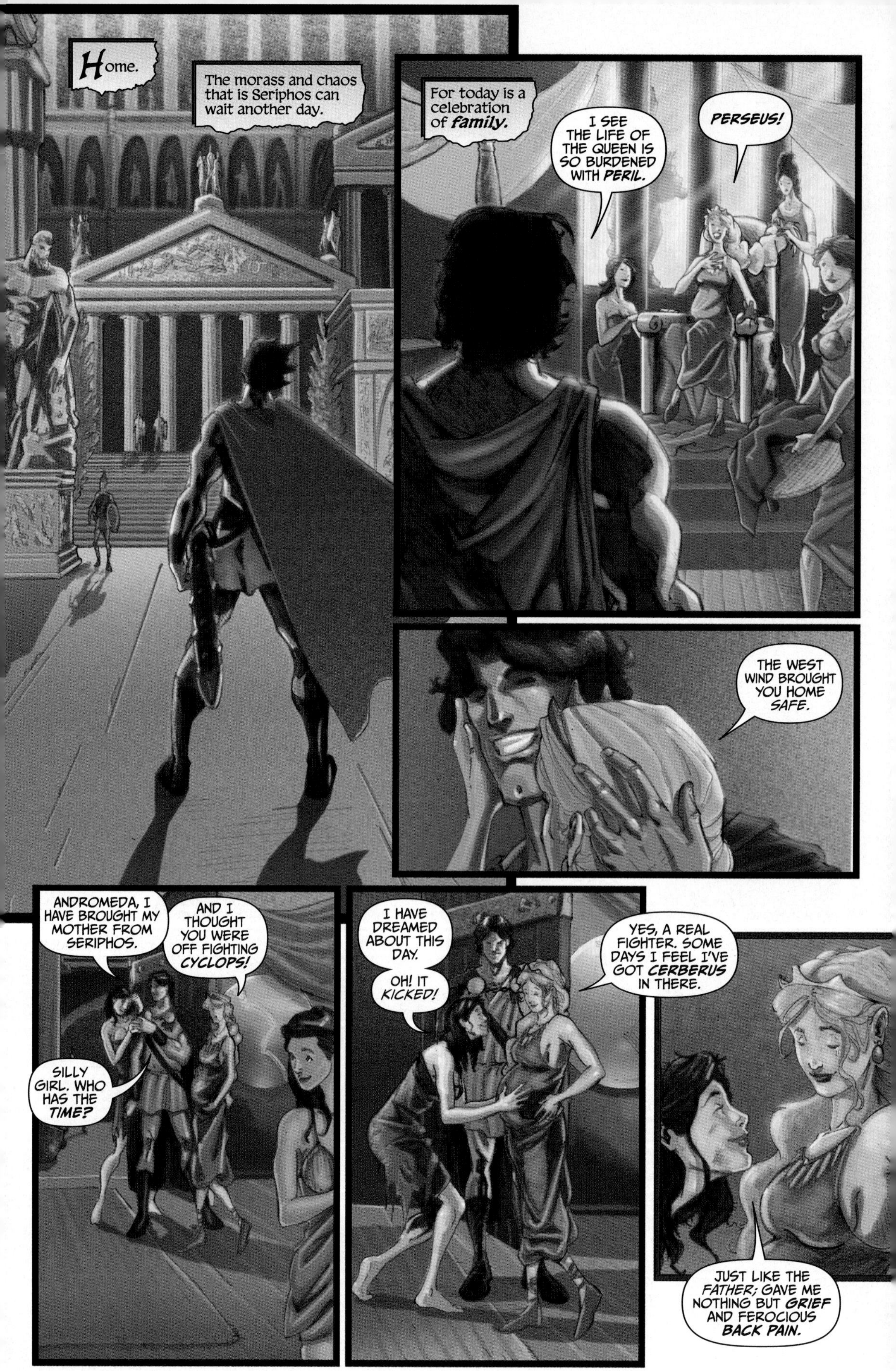
Home.
The morass and chaos that is Seriphos can wait another day.
For today is a celebration of *family.*
I SEE THE LIFE OF THE QUEEN IS SO BURDENED WITH *PERIL.*
PERSEUS!
THE WEST WIND BROUGHT YOU HOME *SAFE.*
ANDROMEDA, I HAVE BROUGHT MY MOTHER FROM SERIPHOS.
AND I THOUGHT YOU WERE OFF FIGHTING *CYCLOPS!*
SILLY GIRL. WHO HAS THE *TIME?*
I HAVE DREAMED ABOUT THIS DAY.
OH! IT *KICKED!*
YES, A REAL FIGHTER. SOME DAYS I FEEL I'VE GOT *CERBERUS* IN THERE.
JUST LIKE THE *FATHER;* GAVE ME NOTHING BUT *GRIEF* AND FEROCIOUS *BACK PAIN.*

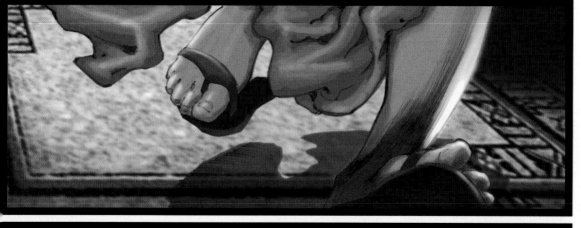

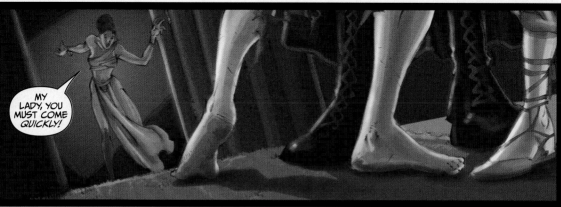

MY LADY, YOU MUST COME QUICKLY!

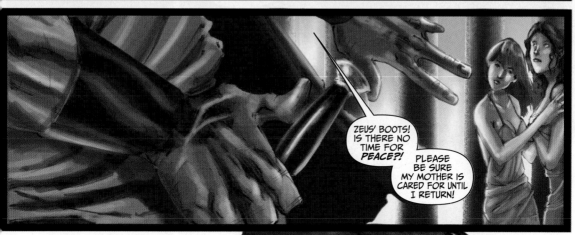

ZEUS' BOOTS! IS THERE NO TIME FOR *PEACE*?!

PLEASE BE SURE MY MOTHER IS CARED FOR UNTIL I RETURN!

There is no way Polydictes could mount a counter-strike so soon.

I left him in the swamps whimpering like a beaten dog.

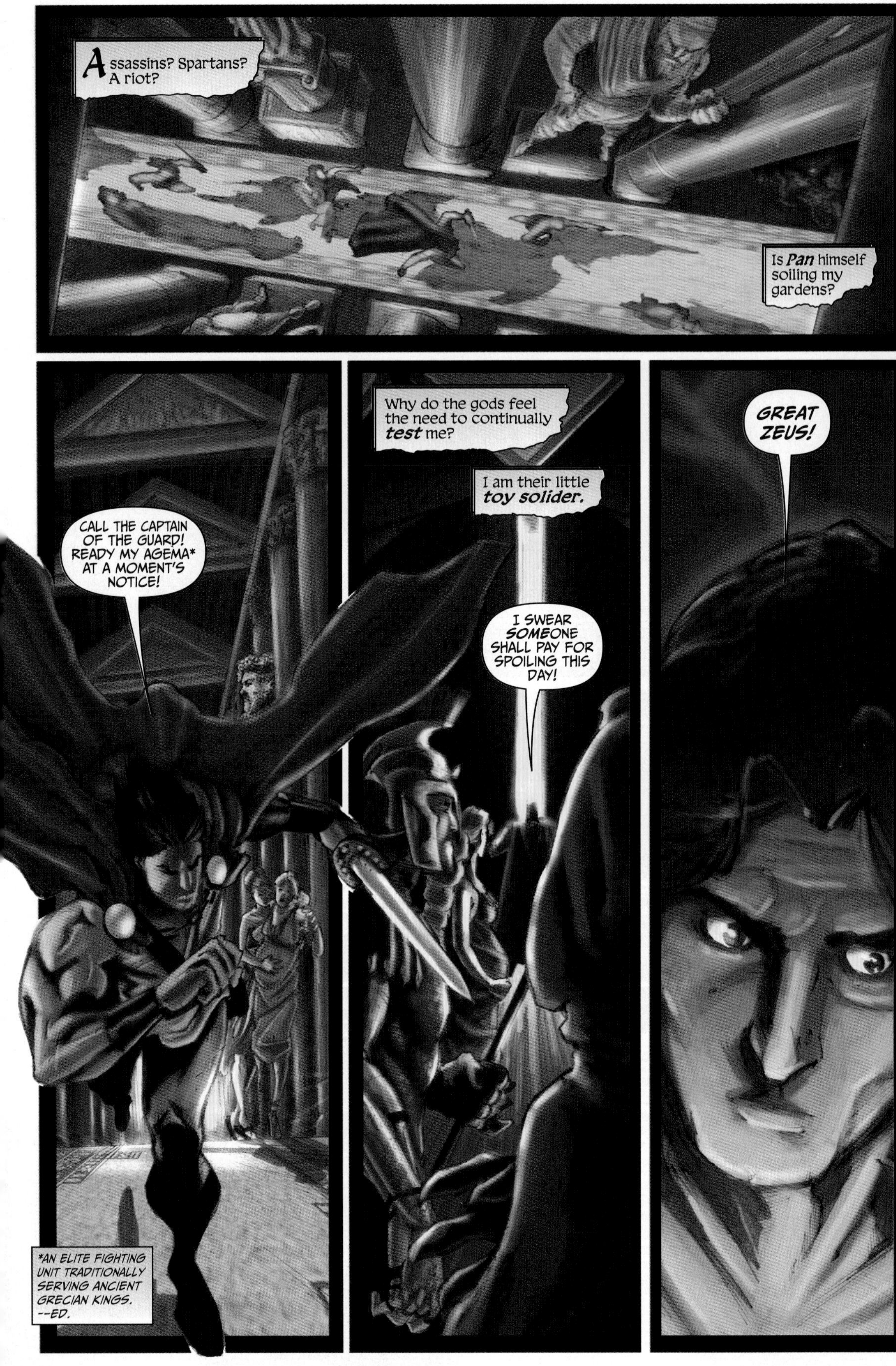
Assassins? Spartans? A riot?
Is Pan himself soiling my gardens?
CALL THE CAPTAIN OF THE GUARD! READY MY AGEMA* AT A MOMENT'S NOTICE!
*AN ELITE FIGHTING UNIT TRADITIONALLY SERVING ANCIENT GRECIAN KINGS. --ED.
Why do the gods feel the need to continually test me?
I am their little toy solider.
I SWEAR SOMEONE SHALL PAY FOR SPOILING THIS DAY!
GREAT ZEUS!

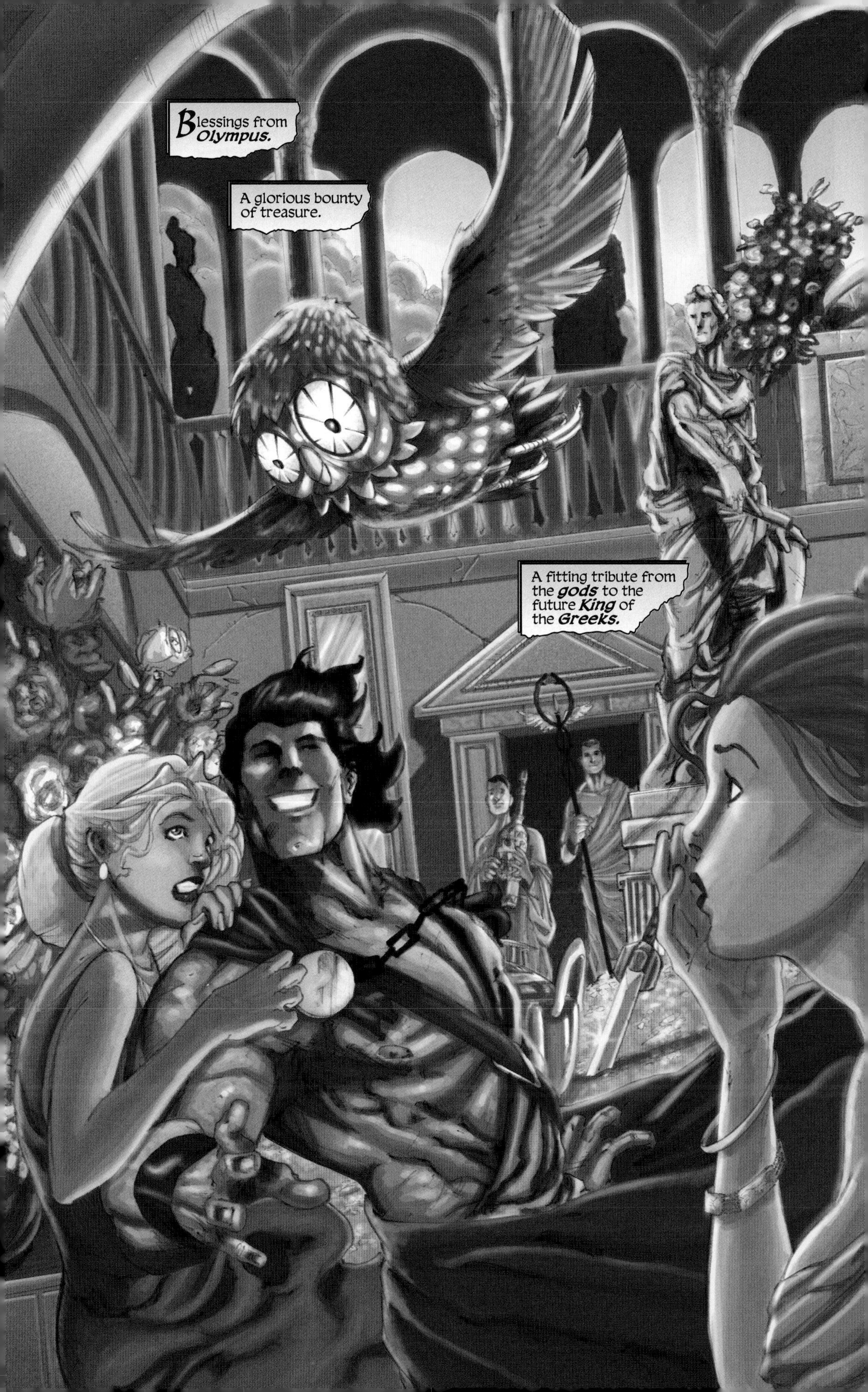
Blessings from Olympus.
A glorious bounty of treasure.
A fitting tribute from the gods to the future King of the Greeks.

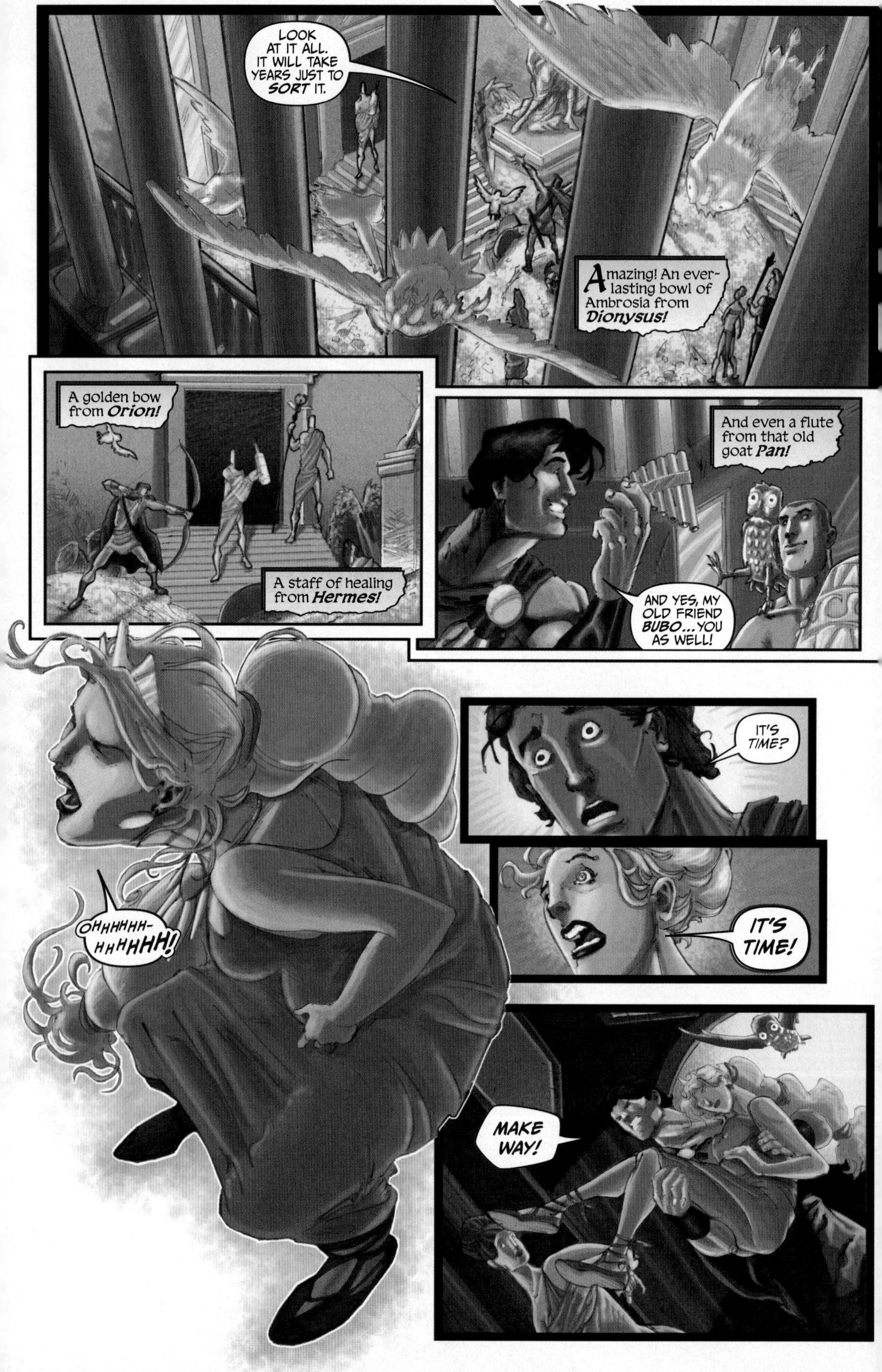
LOOK AT IT ALL. IT WILL TAKE YEARS JUST TO SORT IT.
Amazing! An ever-lasting bowl of Ambrosia from Dionysus!
A golden bow from Orion!
A staff of healing from Hermes!
And even a flute from that old goat Pan!
AND YES, MY OLD FRIEND BUBO... YOU AS WELL!
OHHHHHH-HHHHHH!
IT'S TIME?
IT'S TIME!
MAKE WAY!

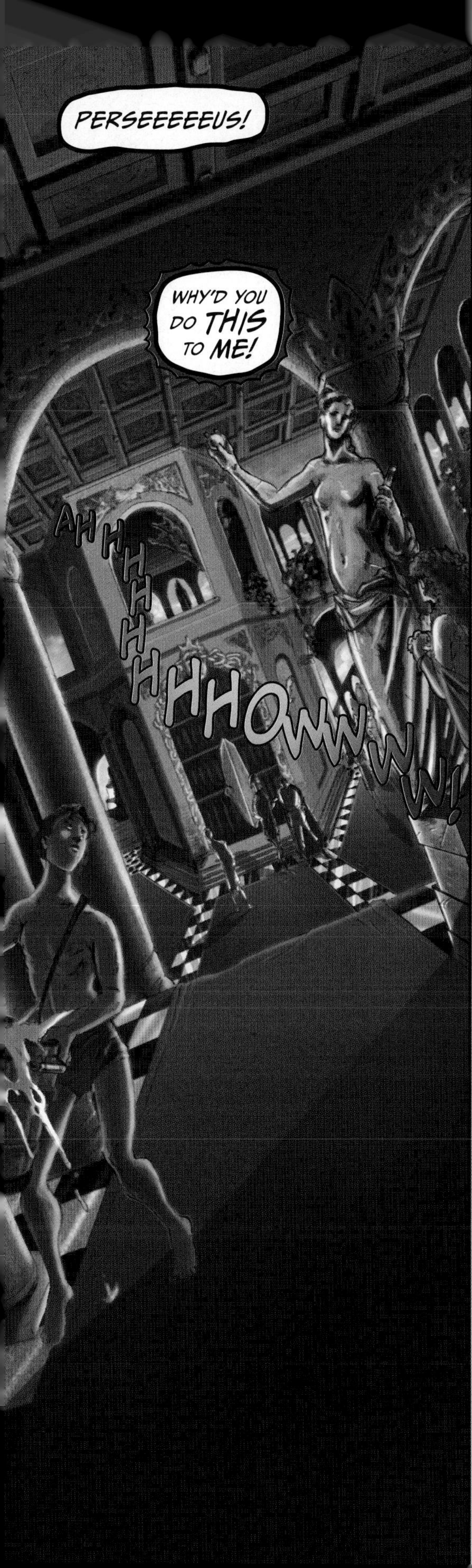
PERSEEEEEUS!
WHY'D YOU DO THIS TO ME!
AHHHHHHHHOWWWWW!

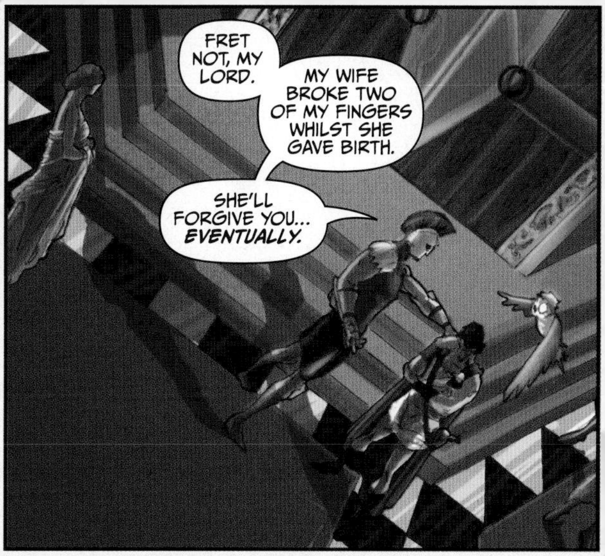
FRET NOT, MY LORD.
MY WIFE BROKE TWO OF MY FINGERS WHILST SHE GAVE BIRTH.
SHE'LL FORGIVE YOU... EVENTUALLY.

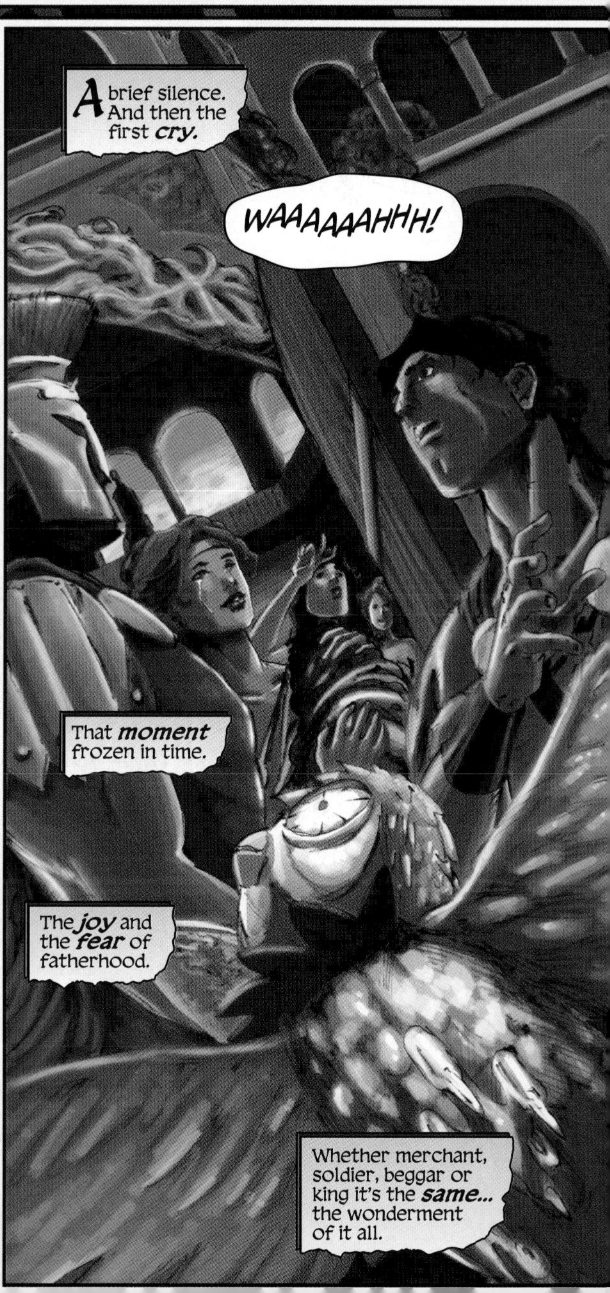
A brief silence. And then the first cry.
WAAAAAAHHH!
That moment frozen in time.
The joy and the fear of fatherhood.
Whether merchant, soldier, beggar or king it's the same... the wonderment of it all.

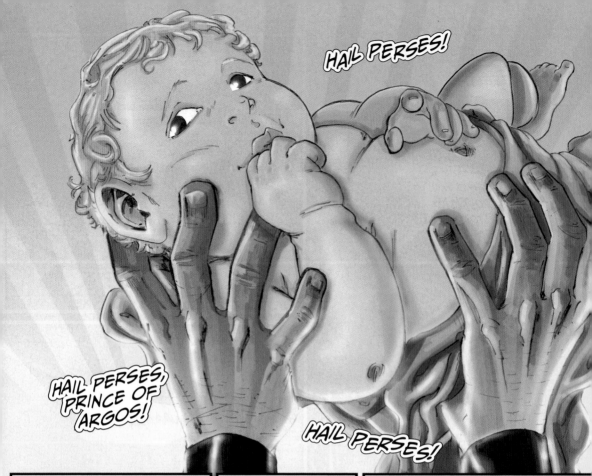

HAIL PERSES!

HAIL PERSES, PRINCE OF ARGOS!

HAIL PERSES!

The citizens of Argos *rejoice*.

LONG LIVE THE PRINCE. HAIL! HAIL!

Though some rejoice for *different* reasons.

INDEED. HAIL THE NEW PRINCE.

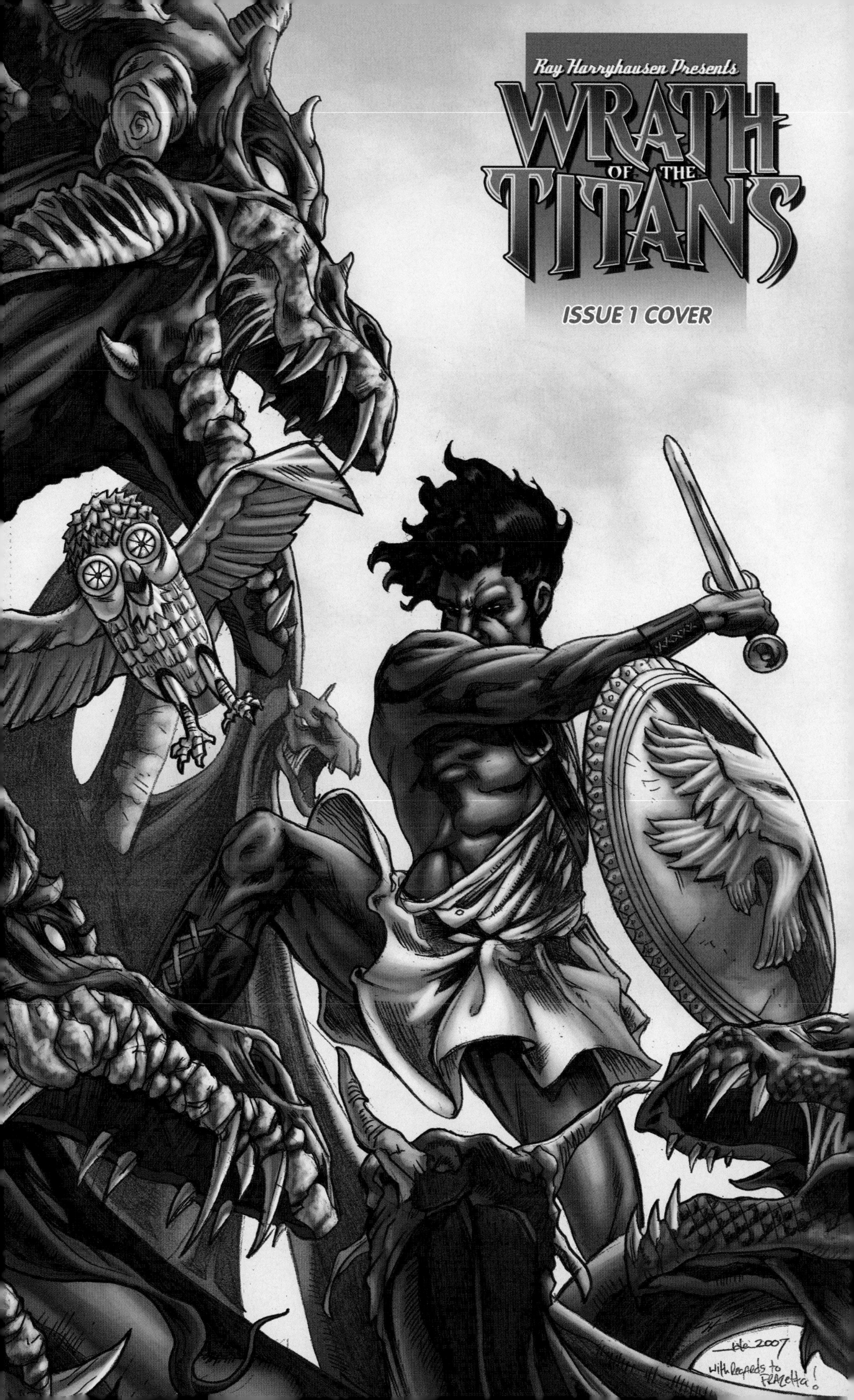
Ray Harryhausen Presents
WRATH OF THE TITANS
ISSUE 1 COVER
2007
With Regards to Frazetta!

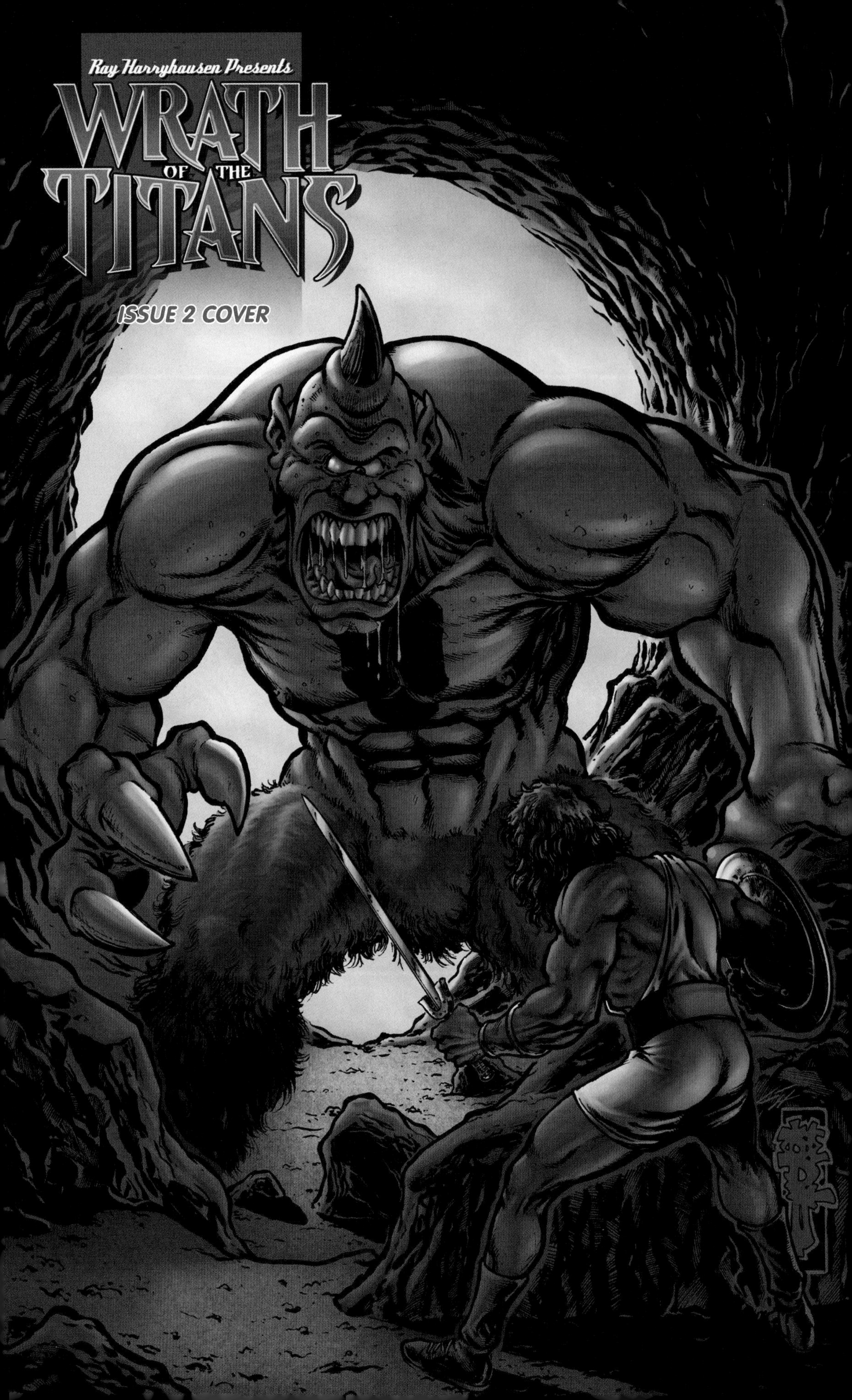
Ray Harryhausen Presents
WRATH OF THE TITANS
ISSUE 2 COVER

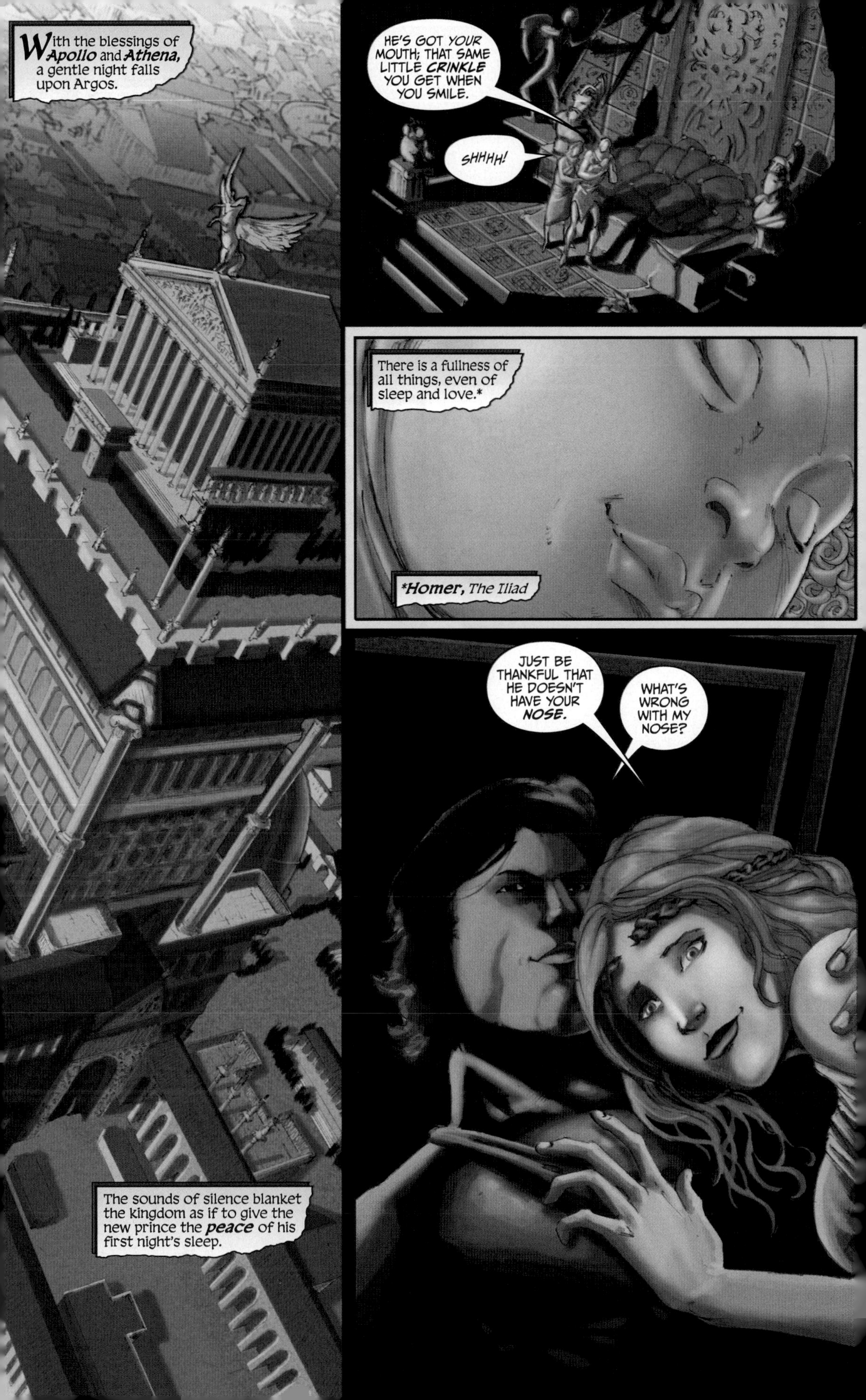
With the blessings of Apollo and Athena, a gentle night falls upon Argos.
The sounds of silence blanket the kingdom as if to give the new prince the peace of his first night's sleep.
HE'S GOT YOUR MOUTH; THAT SAME LITTLE CRINKLE YOU GET WHEN YOU SMILE.
SHHHH!
There is a fullness of all things, even of sleep and love.*
*Homer, The Iliad
JUST BE THANKFUL THAT HE DOESN'T HAVE YOUR NOSE.
WHAT'S WRONG WITH MY NOSE?

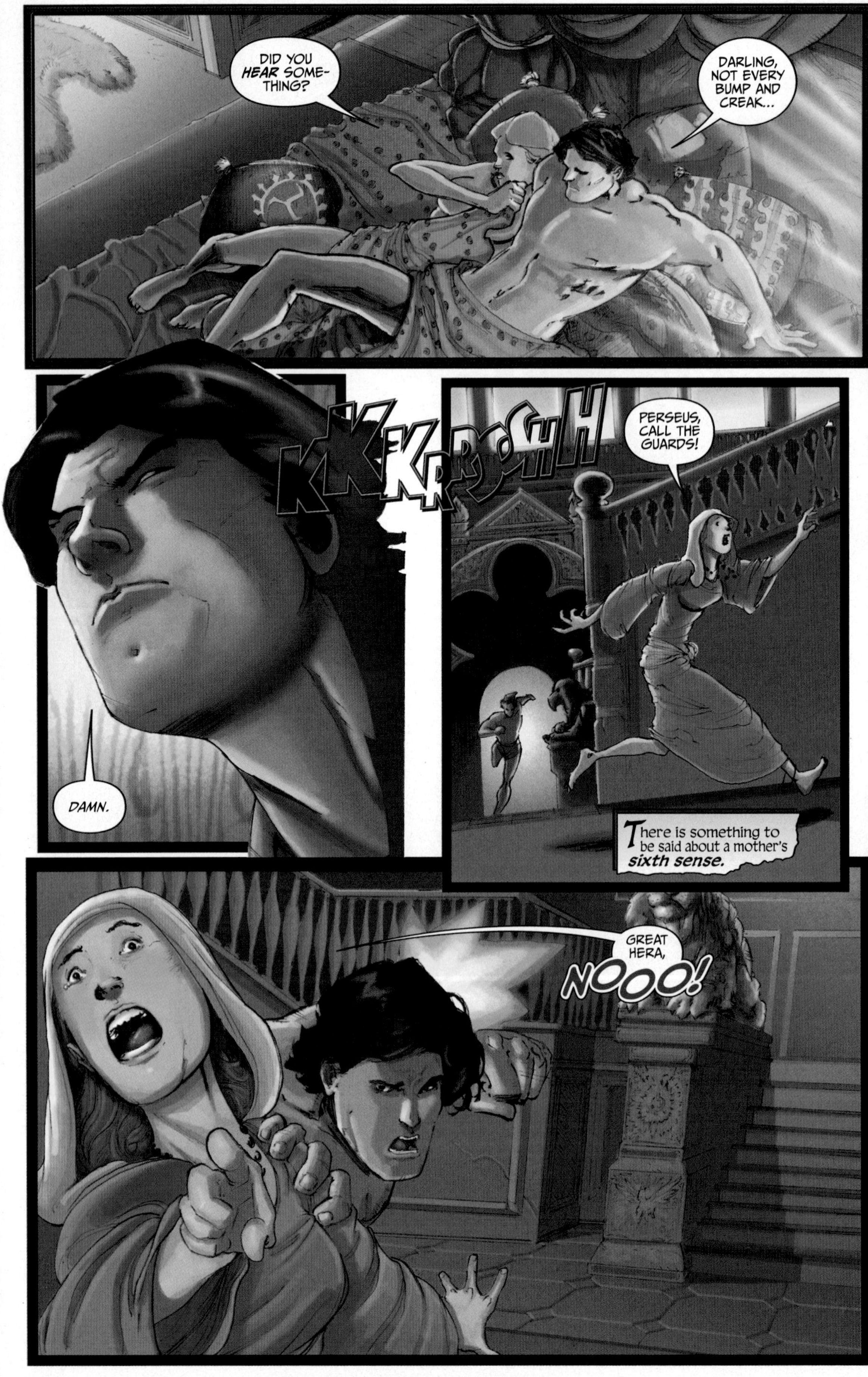
DID YOU HEAR SOME-THING?
DARLING, NOT EVERY BUMP AND CREAK...
DAMN.
KKKRRROSHH
PERSEUS, CALL THE GUARDS!
There is something to be said about a mother's sixth sense.
GREAT HERA, NOOO!

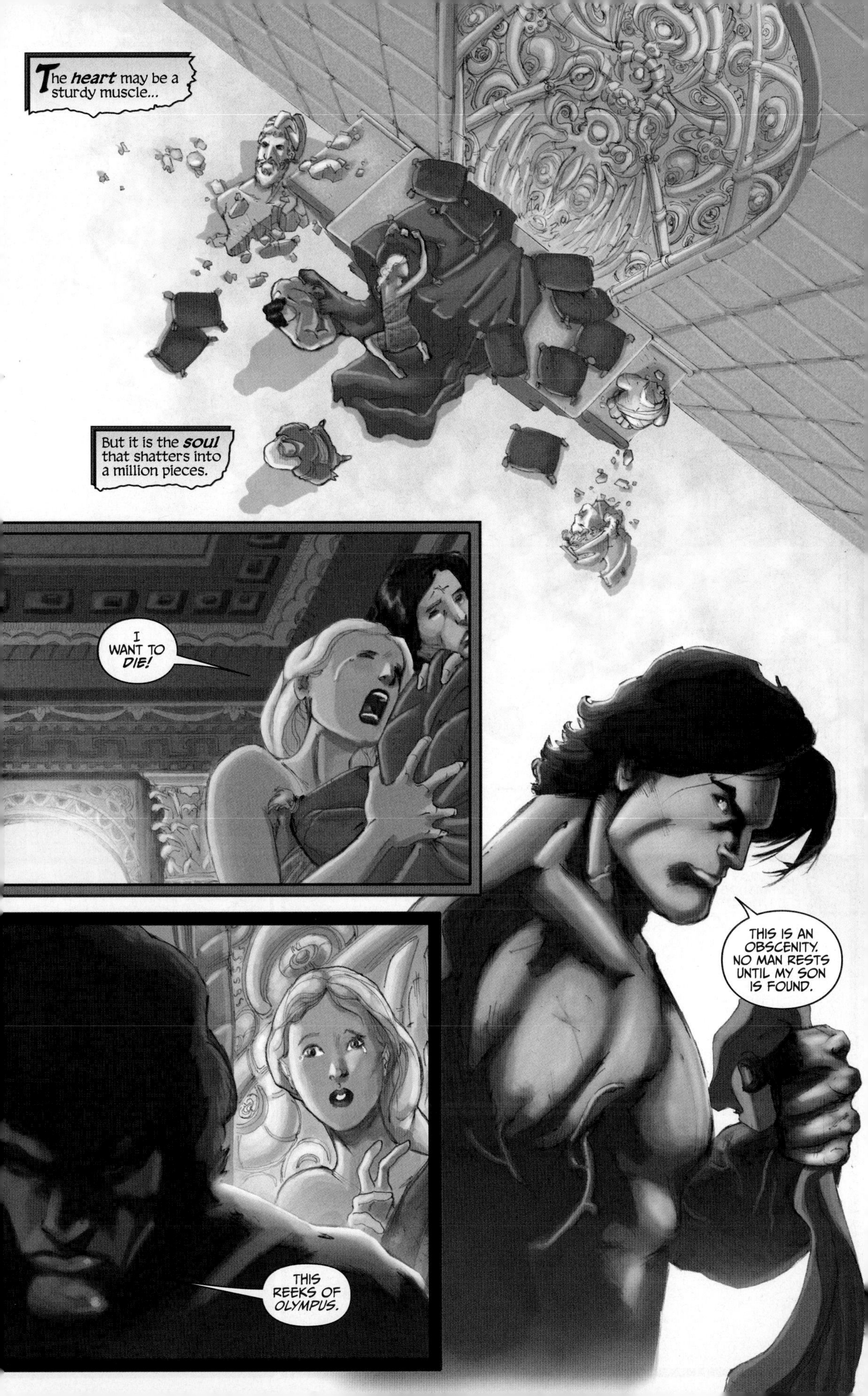
The *heart* may be a sturdy muscle...
But it is the *soul* that shatters into a million pieces.
I WANT TO *DIE!*
THIS IS AN OBSCENITY. NO MAN RESTS UNTIL MY SON IS FOUND.
THIS REEKS OF OLYMPUS.

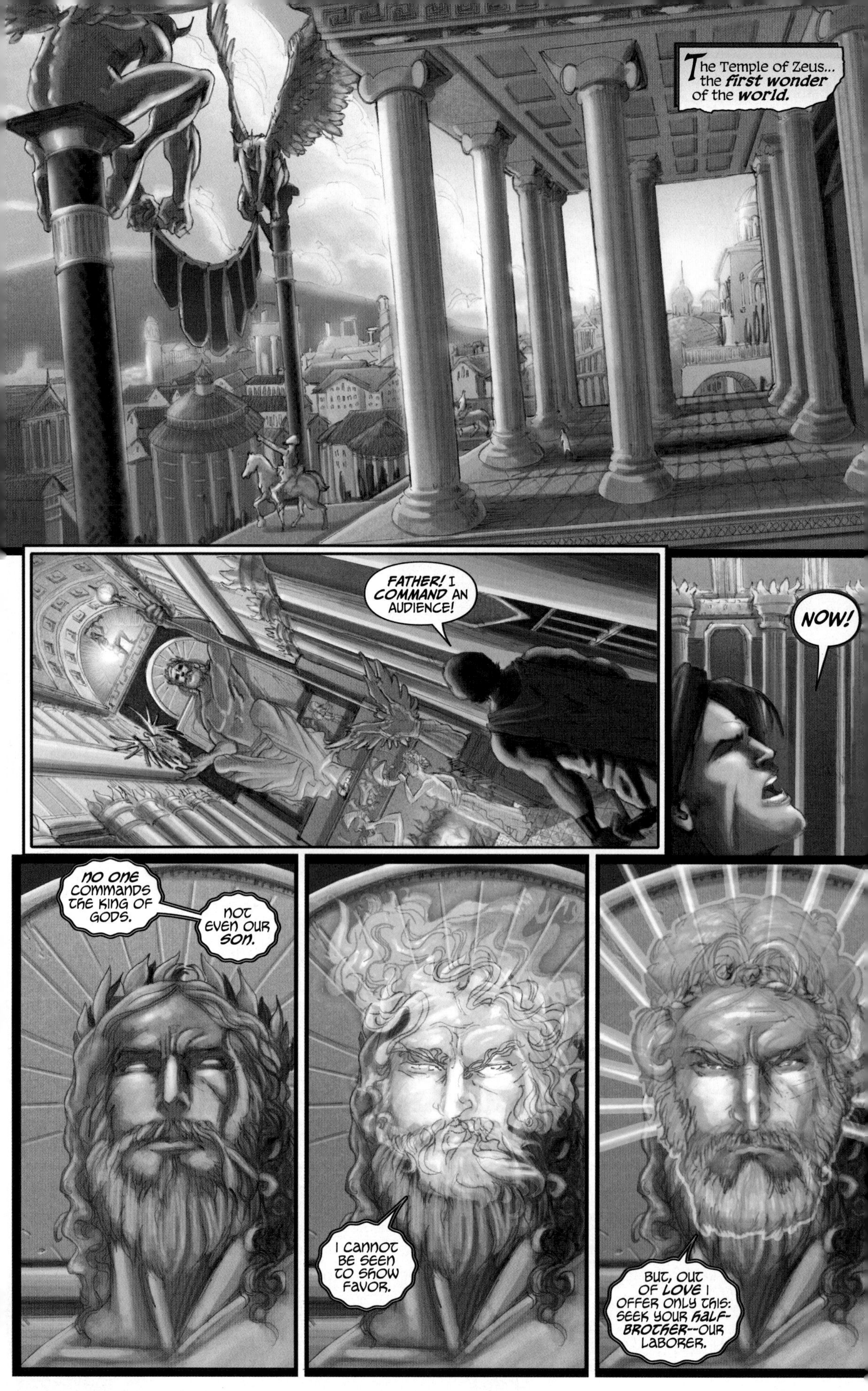
The Temple of Zeus... the first wonder of the world.
FATHER! I COMMAND AN AUDIENCE!
NOW!
NO ONE COMMANDS THE KING OF GODS.
NOT EVEN OUR SON.
I CANNOT BE SEEN TO SHOW FAVOR.
BUT, OUT OF LOVE I OFFER ONLY THIS: SEEK YOUR HALF-BROTHER--OUR LABORER.

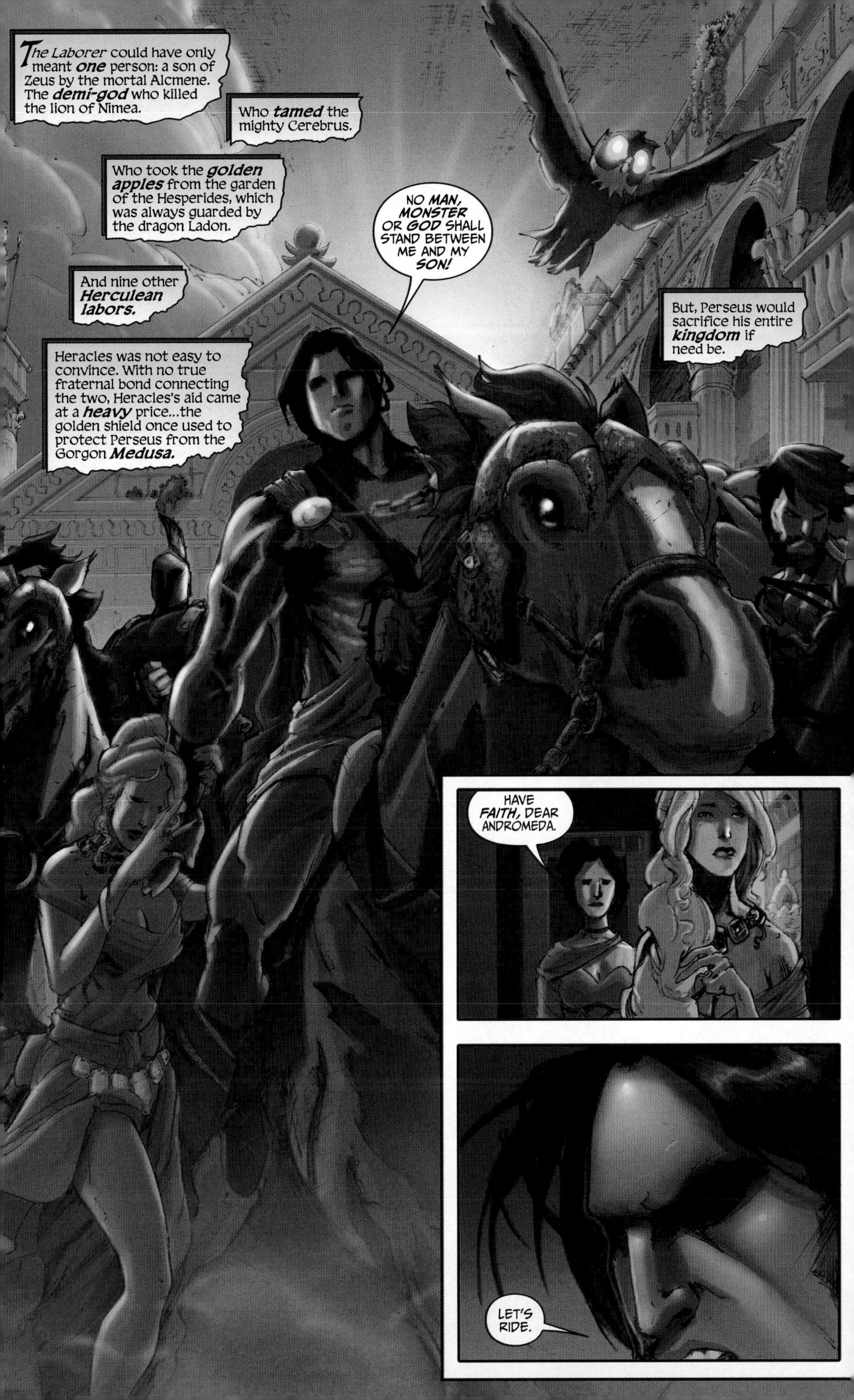

The Laborer could have only meant one person: a son of Zeus by the mortal Alcmene. The demi-god who killed the lion of Nimea.
Who tamed the mighty Cerebrus.
Who took the golden apples from the garden of the Hesperides, which was always guarded by the dragon Ladon.
And nine other Herculean labors.
Heracles was not easy to convince. With no true fraternal bond connecting the two, Heracles's aid came at a heavy price...the golden shield once used to protect Perseus from the Gorgon Medusa.
NO MAN, MONSTER OR GOD SHALL STAND BETWEEN ME AND MY SON!
But, Perseus would sacrifice his entire kingdom if need be.
HAVE FAITH, DEAR ANDROMEDA.
LET'S RIDE.

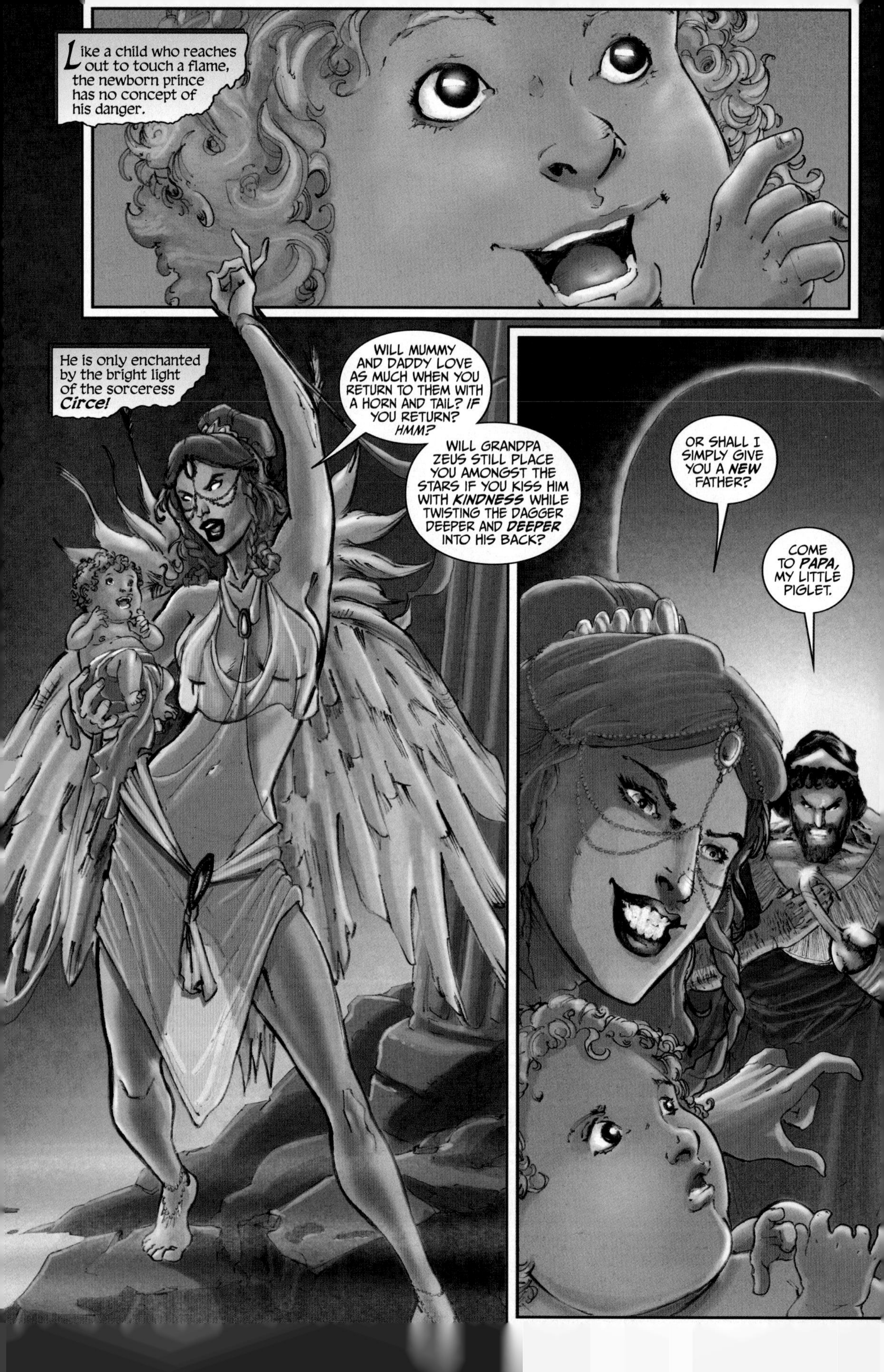
Like a child who reaches out to touch a flame, the newborn prince has no concept of his danger.
He is only enchanted by the bright light of the sorceress *Circe!*
WILL MUMMY AND DADDY LOVE AS MUCH WHEN YOU RETURN TO THEM WITH A HORN AND TAIL? *IF* YOU RETURN? *HMM?*
WILL GRANDPA ZEUS STILL PLACE YOU AMONGST THE STARS IF YOU KISS HIM WITH *KINDNESS* WHILE TWISTING THE DAGGER DEEPER AND *DEEPER* INTO HIS BACK?
OR SHALL I SIMPLY GIVE YOU A *NEW* FATHER?
COME TO *PAPA*, MY LITTLE PIGLET.

HA! A GIANT BOAR? MY *MOTHER* COULD HAVE BESTED A GIANT BOAR. NOW, AN EMPEROR SCORPION, *THAT'S* A MAN'S JOB.

SCORPIONS? NOTHING BUT A *MYTH!* GRIFFINS, ON THE OTHER HAND...

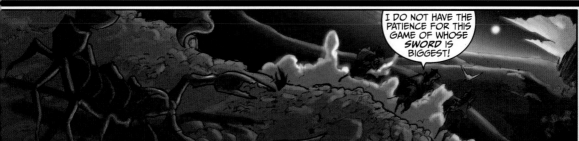

I DO NOT HAVE THE PATIENCE FOR THIS GAME OF WHOSE *SWORD* IS BIGGEST!

YOU, PERSEUS, HAVE BECOME A *KILLJOY!*

YOU WILL FIND I HAVE LOST MORE THAN MY HUMOR.

WE WILL FIND YOUR BOY, BROTHER.

AND THEN WE WILL TOAST HIS RETURN THAT'LL SHAKE OL' BACCHUS *HIMSELF* FROM THE CLOUDS OF OLYMPUS!

QUIET NOW. THE HAGS MAY BE BLIND, BUT THEY'RE NOT *DEAF!*

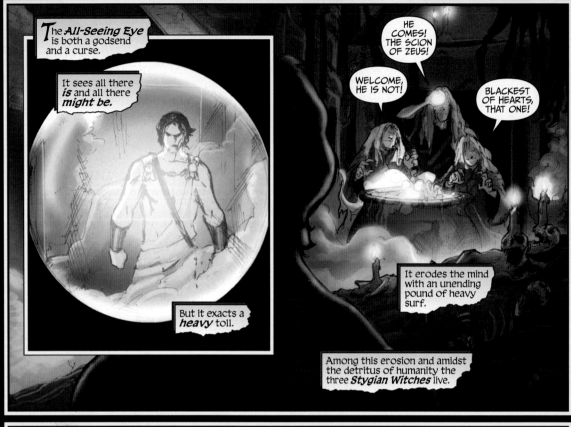

*The **All-Seeing Eye** is both a godsend and a curse.*

*It sees all there **is** and all there **might be.***

*But it exacts a **heavy** toll.*

HE COMES! THE SCION OF ZEUS!

WELCOME, HE IS NOT!

BLACKEST OF HEARTS, THAT ONE!

It erodes the mind with an unending pound of heavy surf.

*Among this erosion and amidst the detritus of humanity the three **Stygian Witches** live.*

BUBO... NOW!

FOOL US ONCE NAUGHTY BOY!

FOOL US TWICE NEVER, NEVER!

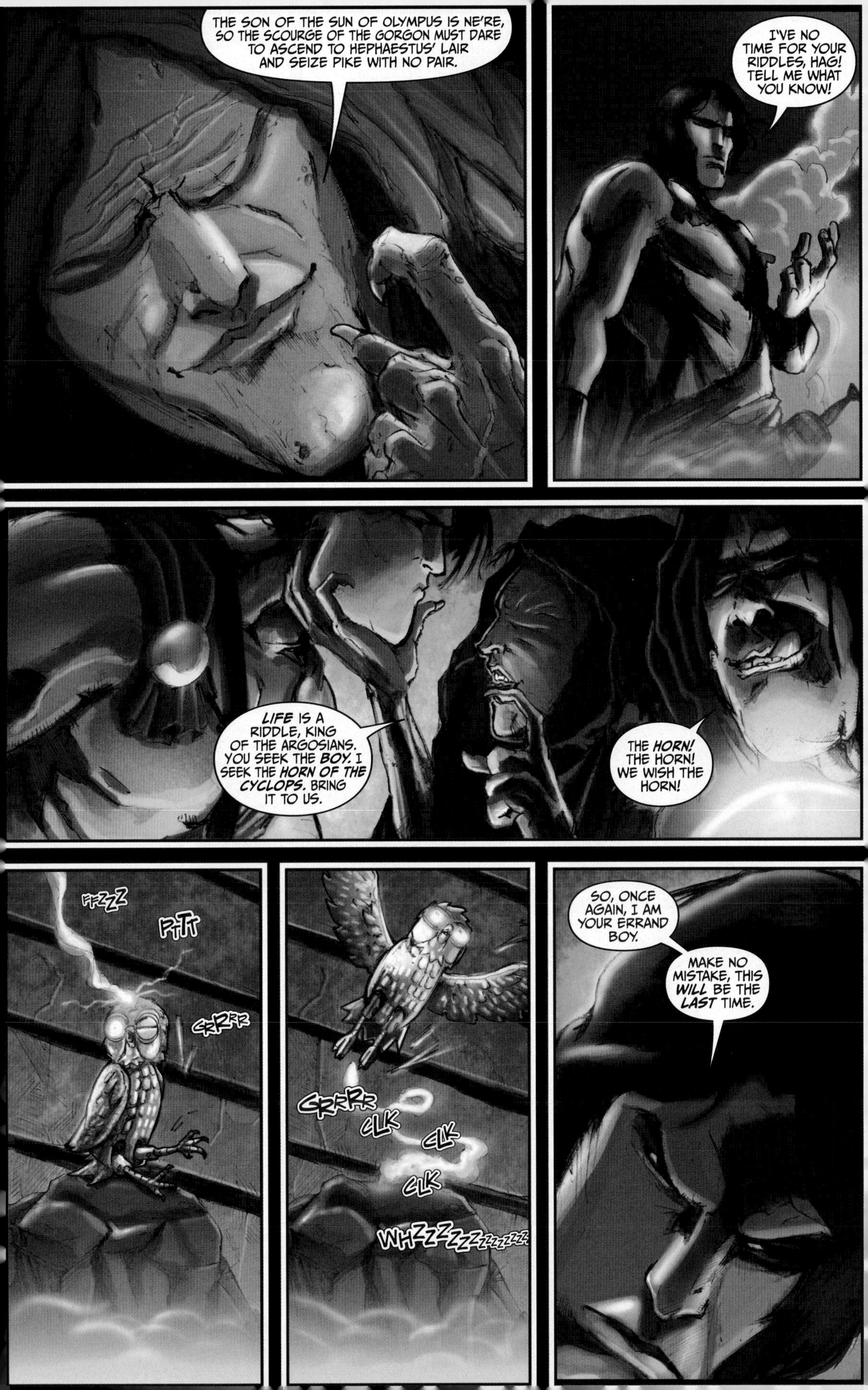
THE SON OF THE SUN OF OLYMPUS IS NE'RE, SO THE SCOURGE OF THE GORGON MUST DARE TO ASCEND TO HEPHAESTUS' LAIR AND SEIZE PIKE WITH NO PAIR.
I'VE NO TIME FOR YOUR RIDDLES, HAG! TELL ME WHAT YOU KNOW!
LIFE IS A RIDDLE, KING OF THE ARGOSIANS. YOU SEEK THE BOY. I SEEK THE HORN OF THE CYCLOPS. BRING IT TO US.
THE HORN! THE HORN! WE WISH THE HORN!
FFZZZ
PTTT
GRRRR
GRRRRR
CLK
CLK
CLK
WHZZZZZZZZZZZ
SO, ONCE AGAIN, I AM YOUR ERRAND BOY.
MAKE NO MISTAKE, THIS WILL BE THE LAST TIME.

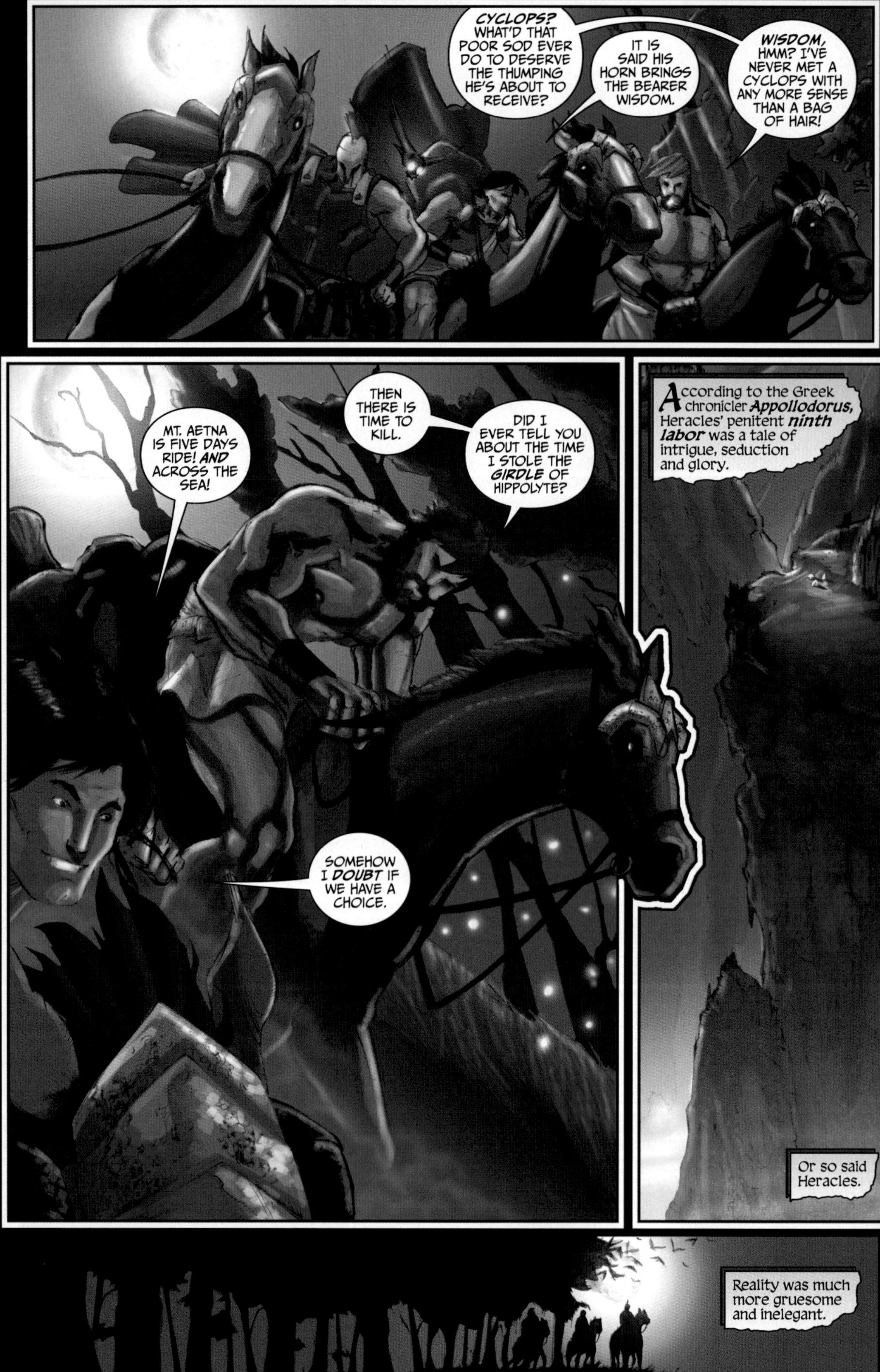
CYCLOPS? WHAT'D THAT POOR SOD EVER DO TO DESERVE THE THUMPING HE'S ABOUT TO RECEIVE?
IT IS SAID HIS HORN BRINGS THE BEARER WISDOM.
WISDOM, HMM? I'VE NEVER MET A CYCLOPS WITH ANY MORE SENSE THAN A BAG OF HAIR!
MT. AETNA IS FIVE DAYS RIDE! AND ACROSS THE SEA!
THEN THERE IS TIME TO KILL.
DID I EVER TELL YOU ABOUT THE TIME I STOLE THE GIRDLE OF HIPPOLYTE?
SOMEHOW I DOUBT IF WE HAVE A CHOICE.
According to the Greek chronicler Appollodorus, Heracles' penitent ninth labor was a tale of intrigue, seduction and glory.
Or so said Heracles.
Reality was much more gruesome and inelegant.

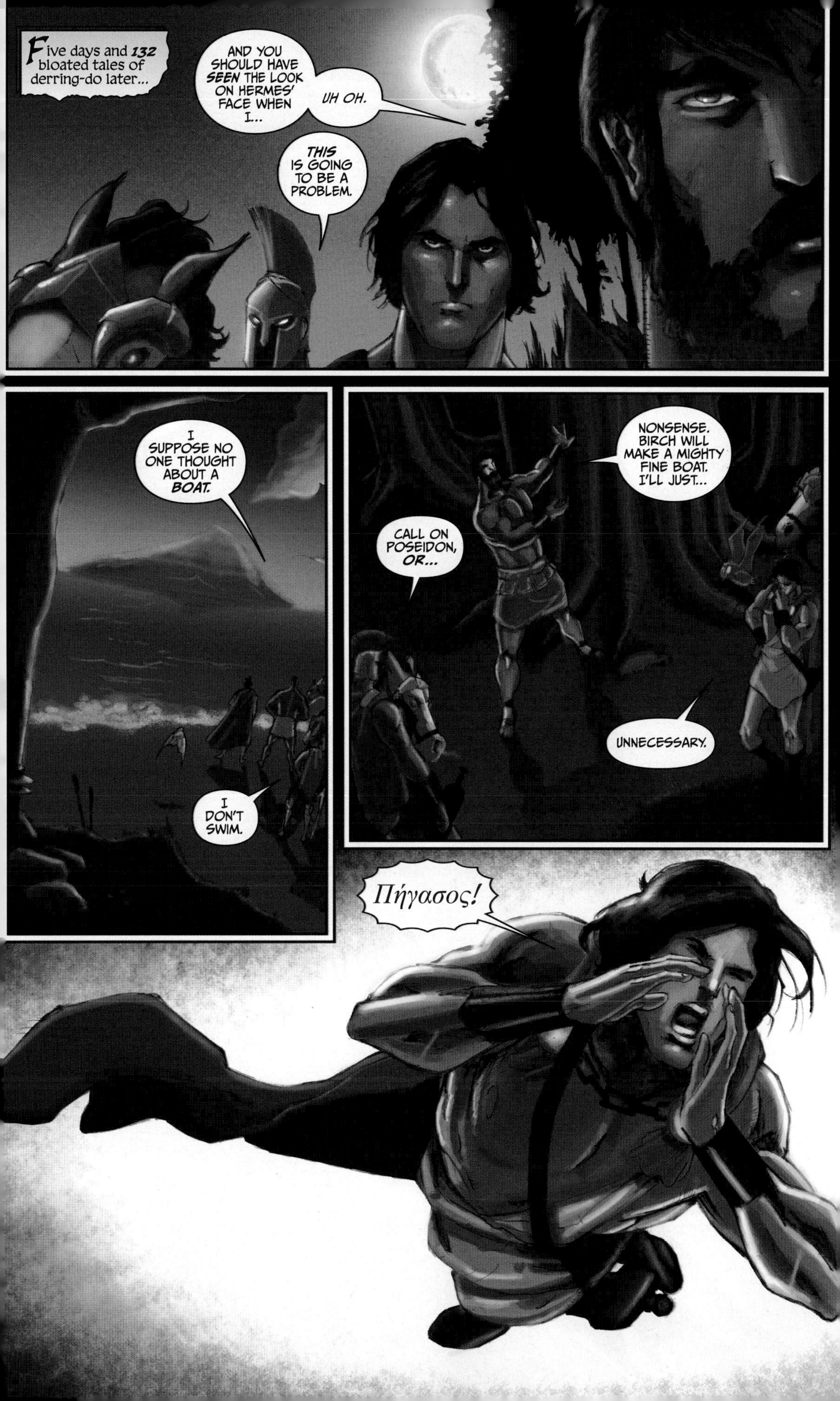
Five days and 132 bloated tales of derring-do later...
AND YOU SHOULD HAVE SEEN THE LOOK ON HERMES' FACE WHEN I...
UH OH.
THIS IS GOING TO BE A PROBLEM.
I SUPPOSE NO ONE THOUGHT ABOUT A BOAT.
I DON'T SWIM.
NONSENSE. BIRCH WILL MAKE A MIGHTY FINE BOAT. I'LL JUST...
CALL ON POSEIDON, OR...
UNNECESSARY.
Πήγασος!

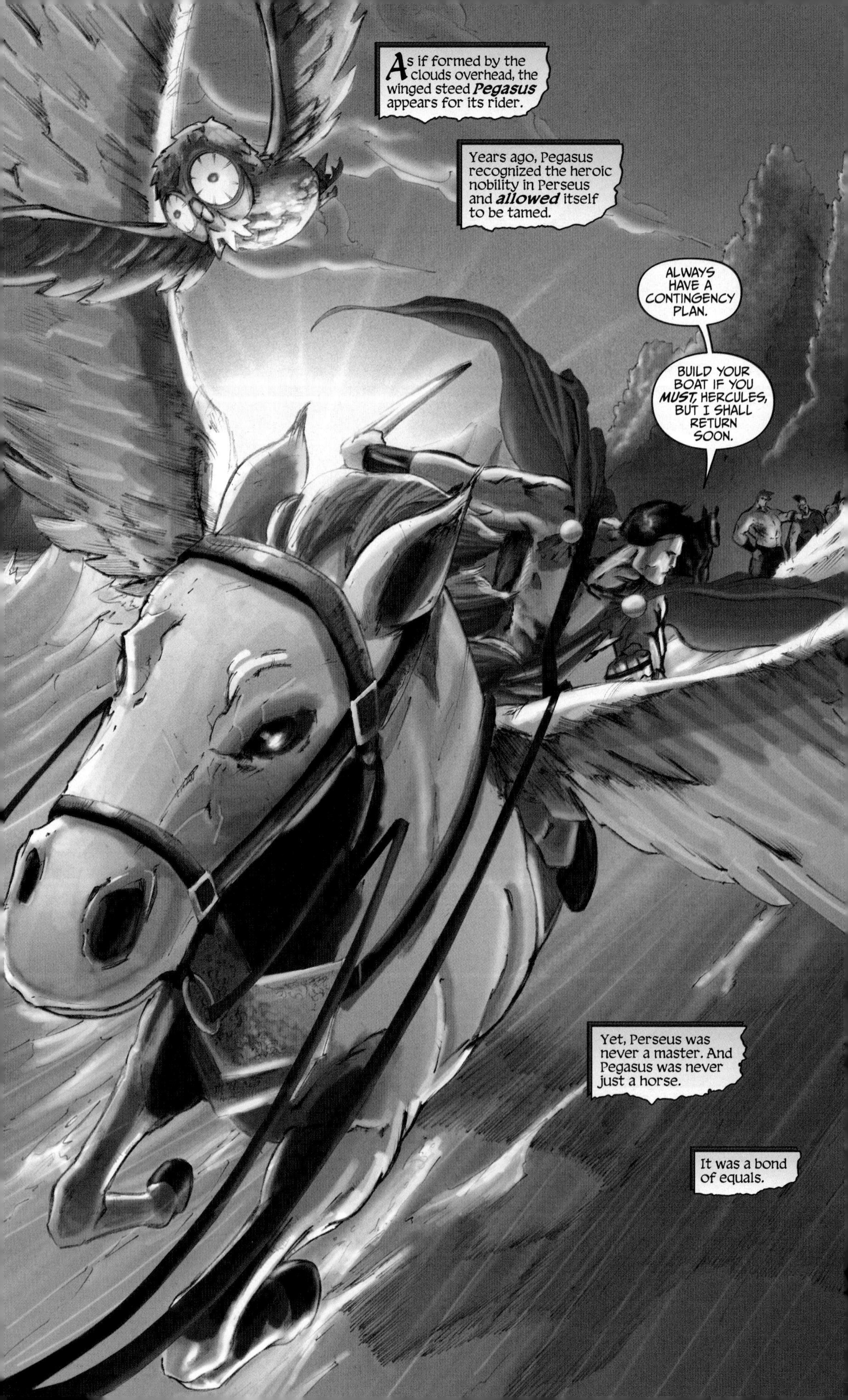
As if formed by the clouds overhead, the winged steed *Pegasus* appears for its rider.
Years ago, Pegasus recognized the heroic nobility in Perseus and *allowed* itself to be tamed.
ALWAYS HAVE A CONTINGENCY PLAN.
BUILD YOUR BOAT IF YOU *MUST,* HERCULES, BUT I SHALL RETURN SOON.
Yet, Perseus was never a master. And Pegasus was never just a horse.
It was a bond of equals.

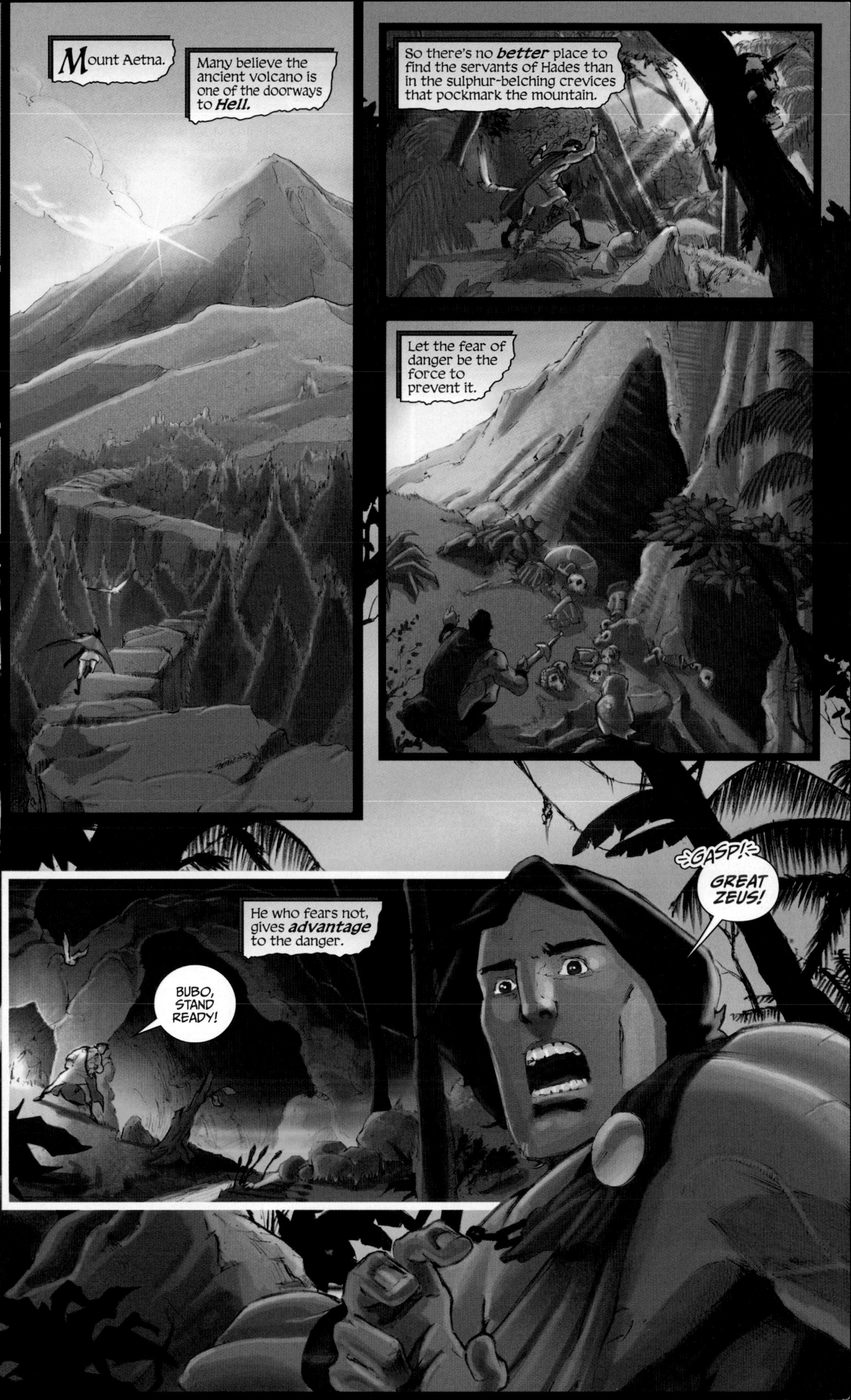
Mount Aetna.
Many believe the ancient volcano is one of the doorways to **Hell.**
So there's no **better** place to find the servants of Hades than in the sulphur-belching crevices that pockmark the mountain.
Let the fear of danger be the force to prevent it.
He who fears not, gives **advantage** to the danger.
BUBO, STAND READY!
GASP!
GREAT ZEUS!

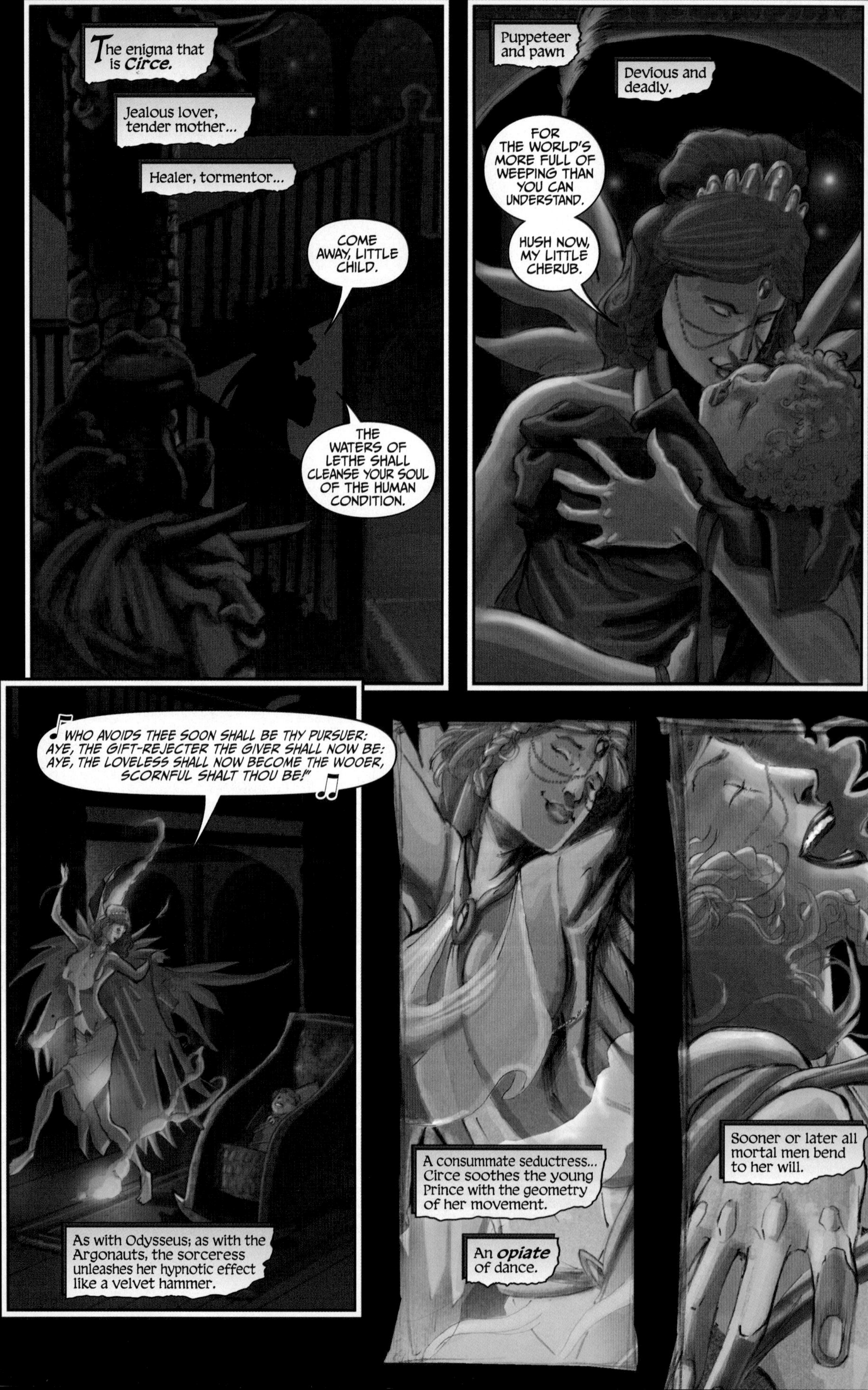
The enigma that is Circe.
Jealous lover, tender mother...
Healer, tormentor...
COME AWAY, LITTLE CHILD.
THE WATERS OF LETHE SHALL CLEANSE YOUR SOUL OF THE HUMAN CONDITION.
Puppeteer and pawn
Devious and deadly.
FOR THE WORLD'S MORE FULL OF WEEPING THAN YOU CAN UNDERSTAND.
HUSH NOW, MY LITTLE CHERUB.
WHO AVOIDS THEE SOON SHALL BE THY PURSUER: AYE, THE GIFT-REJECTER THE GIVER SHALL NOW BE: AYE, THE LOVELESS SHALL NOW BECOME THE WOOER, SCORNFUL SHALT THOU BE!"
As with Odysseus; as with the Argonauts, the sorceress unleashes her hypnotic effect like a velvet hammer.
A consummate seductress... Circe soothes the young Prince with the geometry of her movement.
An opiate of dance.
Sooner or later all mortal men bend to her will.

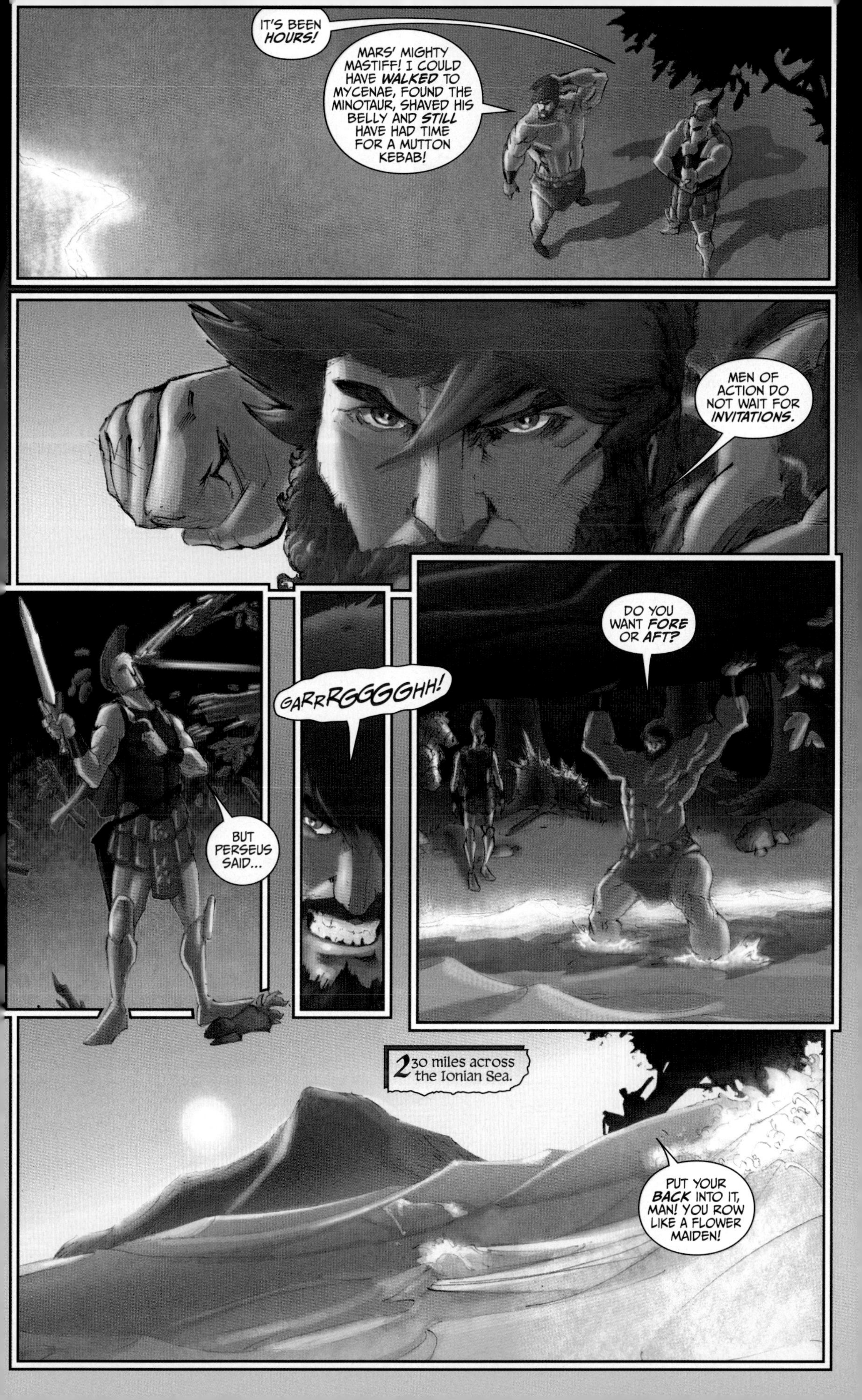
IT'S BEEN HOURS!
MARS' MIGHTY MASTIFF! I COULD HAVE WALKED TO MYCENAE, FOUND THE MINOTAUR, SHAVED HIS BELLY AND STILL HAVE HAD TIME FOR A MUTTON KEBAB!
MEN OF ACTION DO NOT WAIT FOR INVITATIONS.
BUT PERSEUS SAID...
GARRRGGGGHH!
DO YOU WANT FORE OR AFT?
230 miles across the Ionian Sea.
PUT YOUR BACK INTO IT, MAN! YOU ROW LIKE A FLOWER MAIDEN!

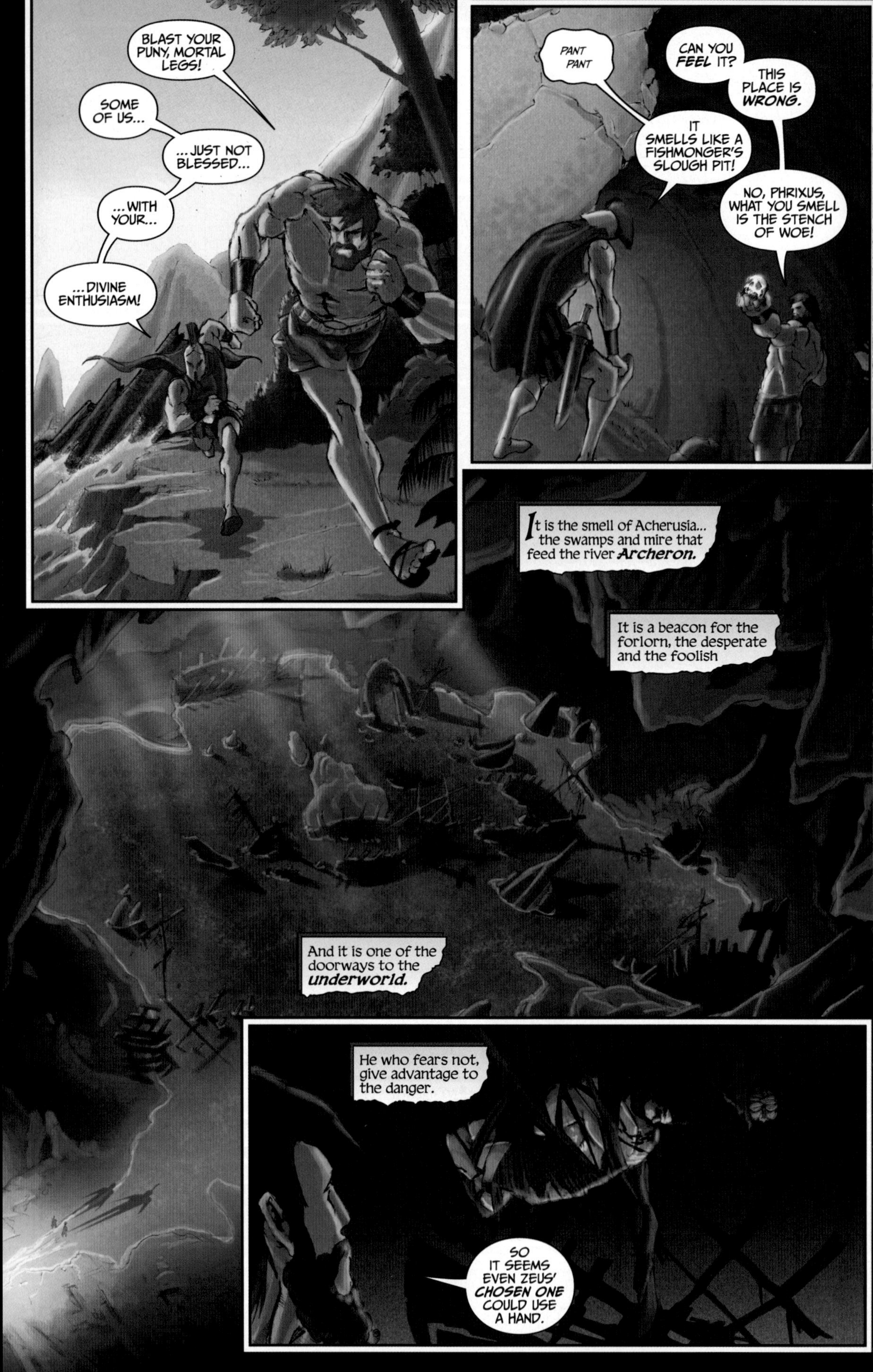
BLAST YOUR PUNY, MORTAL LEGS!
SOME OF US...
...JUST NOT BLESSED...
...WITH YOUR...
...DIVINE ENTHUSIASM!
PANT PANT
CAN YOU FEEL IT?
THIS PLACE IS WRONG.
IT SMELLS LIKE A FISHMONGER'S SLOUGH PIT!
NO, PHRIXUS, WHAT YOU SMELL IS THE STENCH OF WOE!
It is the smell of Acherusia... the swamps and mire that feed the river Archeron.
It is a beacon for the forlorn, the desperate and the foolish
And it is one of the doorways to the underworld.
He who fears not, give advantage to the danger.
SO IT SEEMS EVEN ZEUS' CHOSEN ONE COULD USE A HAND.

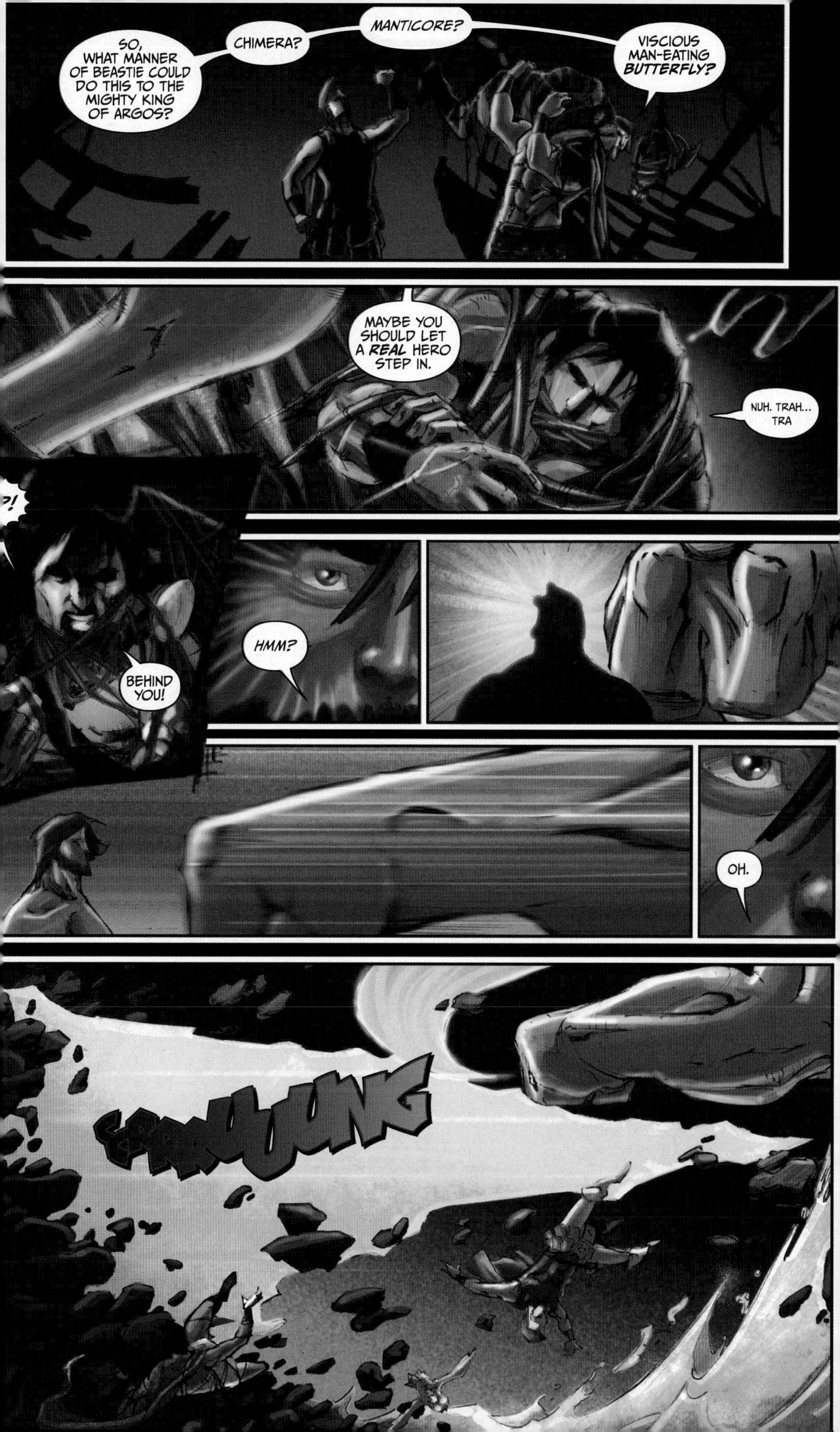
SO, WHAT MANNER OF BEASTIE COULD DO THIS TO THE MIGHTY KING OF ARGOS?
CHIMERA?
MANTICORE?
VISCIOUS MAN-EATING BUTTERFLY?
MAYBE YOU SHOULD LET A REAL HERO STEP IN.
NUH. TRAH... TRA
BEHIND YOU!
HMM?
OH.

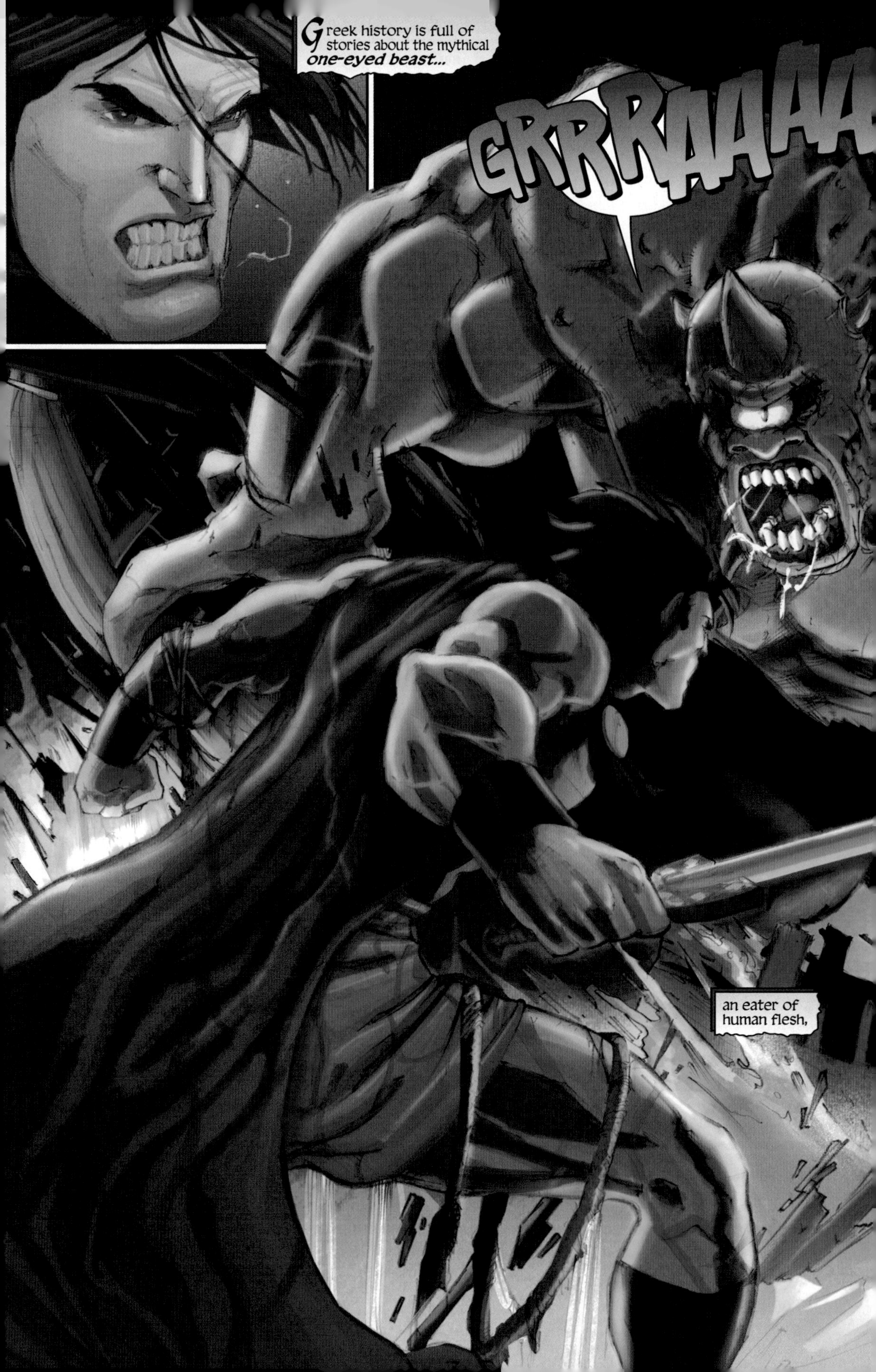
Greek history is full of stories about the mythical one-eyed beast...
GRRRAAAA
an eater of human flesh,

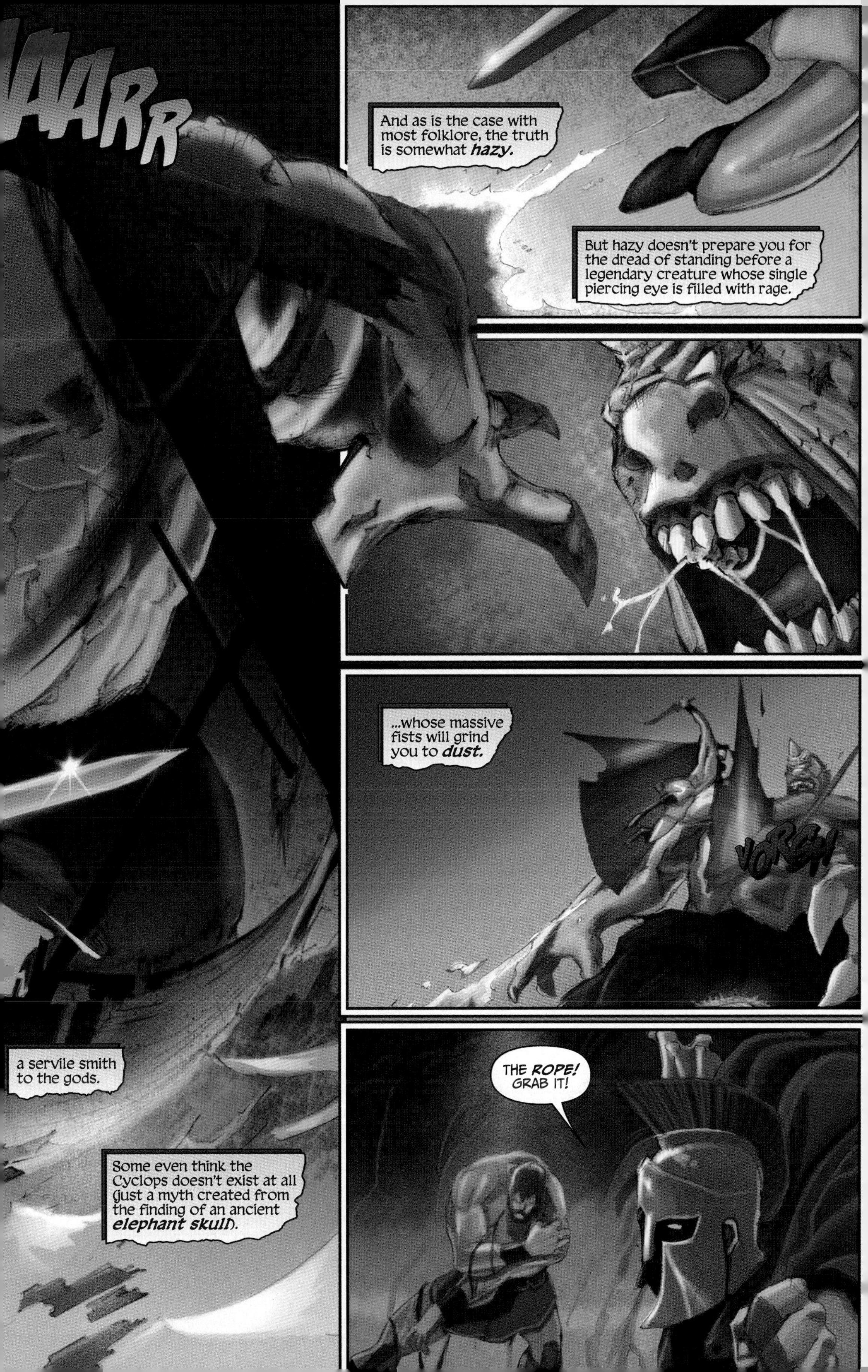
AARR
a servile smith to the gods.
Some even think the Cyclops doesn't exist at all (just a myth created from the finding of an ancient *elephant skull*).
And as is the case with most folklore, the truth is somewhat *hazy.*
But hazy doesn't prepare you for the dread of standing before a legendary creature whose single piercing eye is filled with rage.
...whose massive fists will grind you to *dust.*
VORGH
THE *ROPE!* GRAB IT!

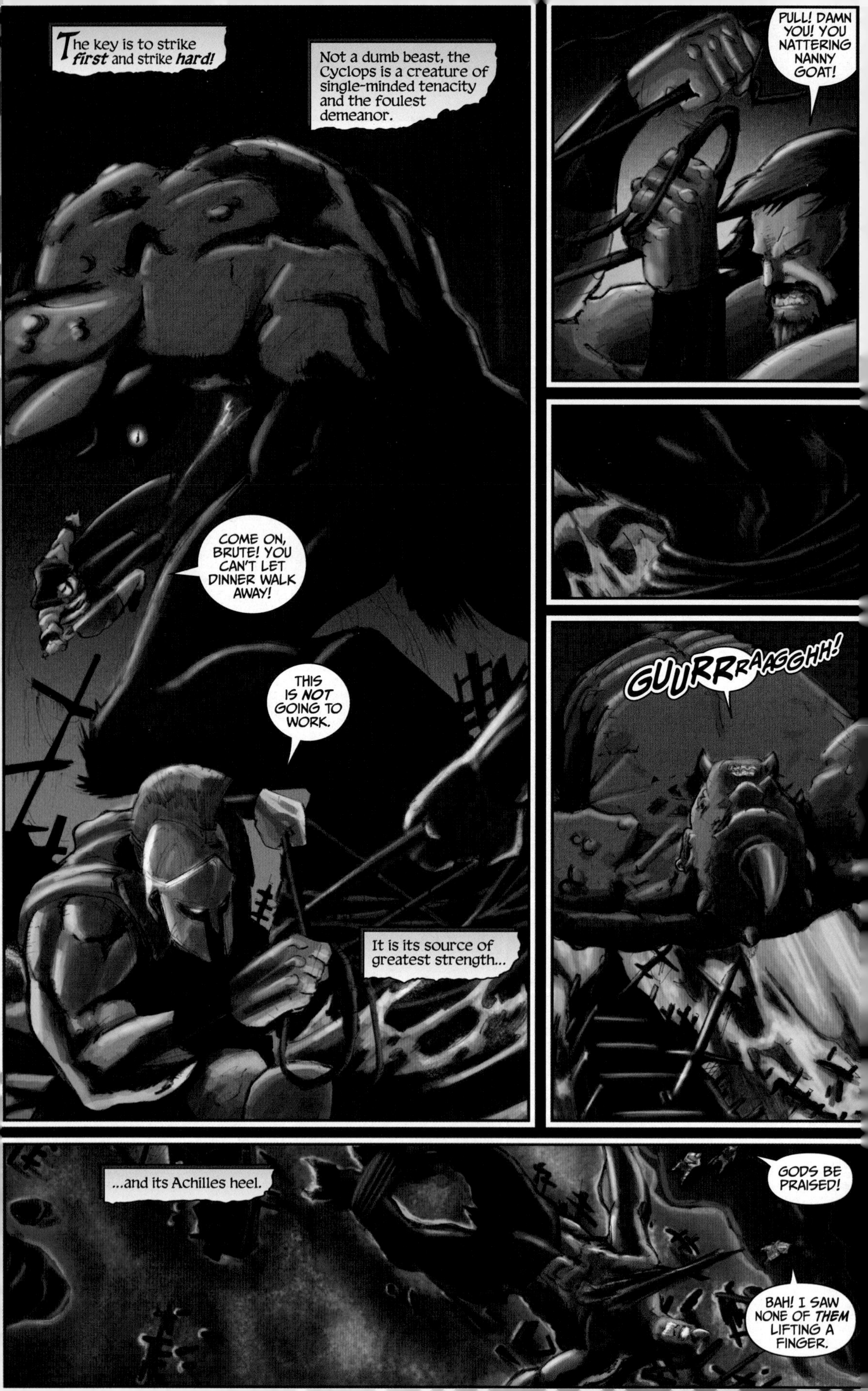
The key is to strike *first* and strike *hard!*
Not a dumb beast, the Cyclops is a creature of single-minded tenacity and the foulest demeanor.
COME ON, BRUTE! YOU CAN'T LET DINNER WALK AWAY!
THIS IS *NOT* GOING TO WORK.
It is its source of greatest strength...
PULL! DAMN YOU! YOU NATTERING NANNY GOAT!
GUURRRAAGGHH!
...and its Achilles heel.
GODS BE PRAISED!
BAH! I SAW NONE OF *THEM* LIFTING A FINGER.

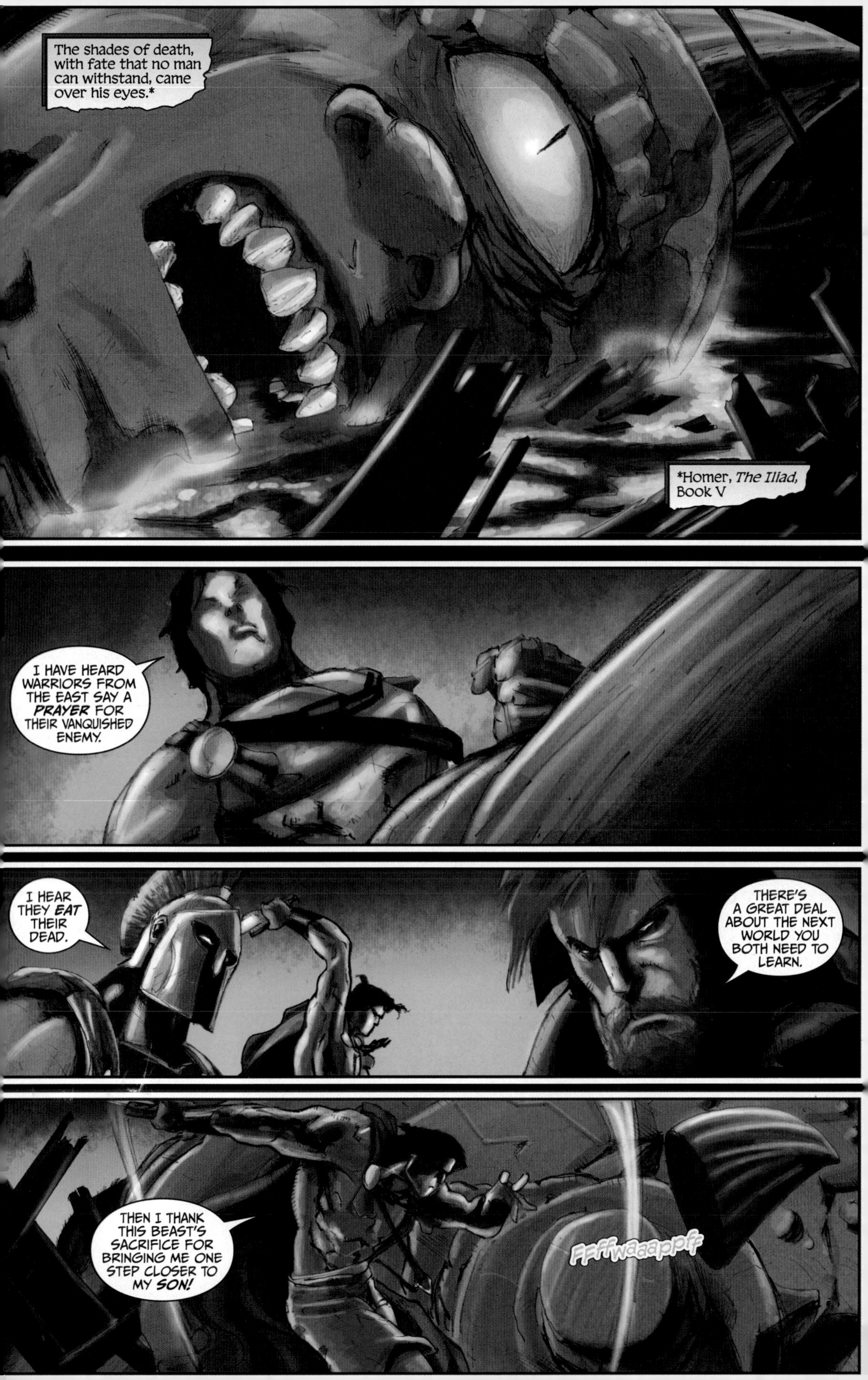
The shades of death, with fate that no man can withstand, came over his eyes.*
*Homer, The Iliad, Book V
I HAVE HEARD WARRIORS FROM THE EAST SAY A PRAYER FOR THEIR VANQUISHED ENEMY.
I HEAR THEY EAT THEIR DEAD.
THERE'S A GREAT DEAL ABOUT THE NEXT WORLD YOU BOTH NEED TO LEARN.
THEN I THANK THIS BEAST'S SACRIFICE FOR BRINGING ME ONE STEP CLOSER TO MY SON!
FFFFWAAAPPFF

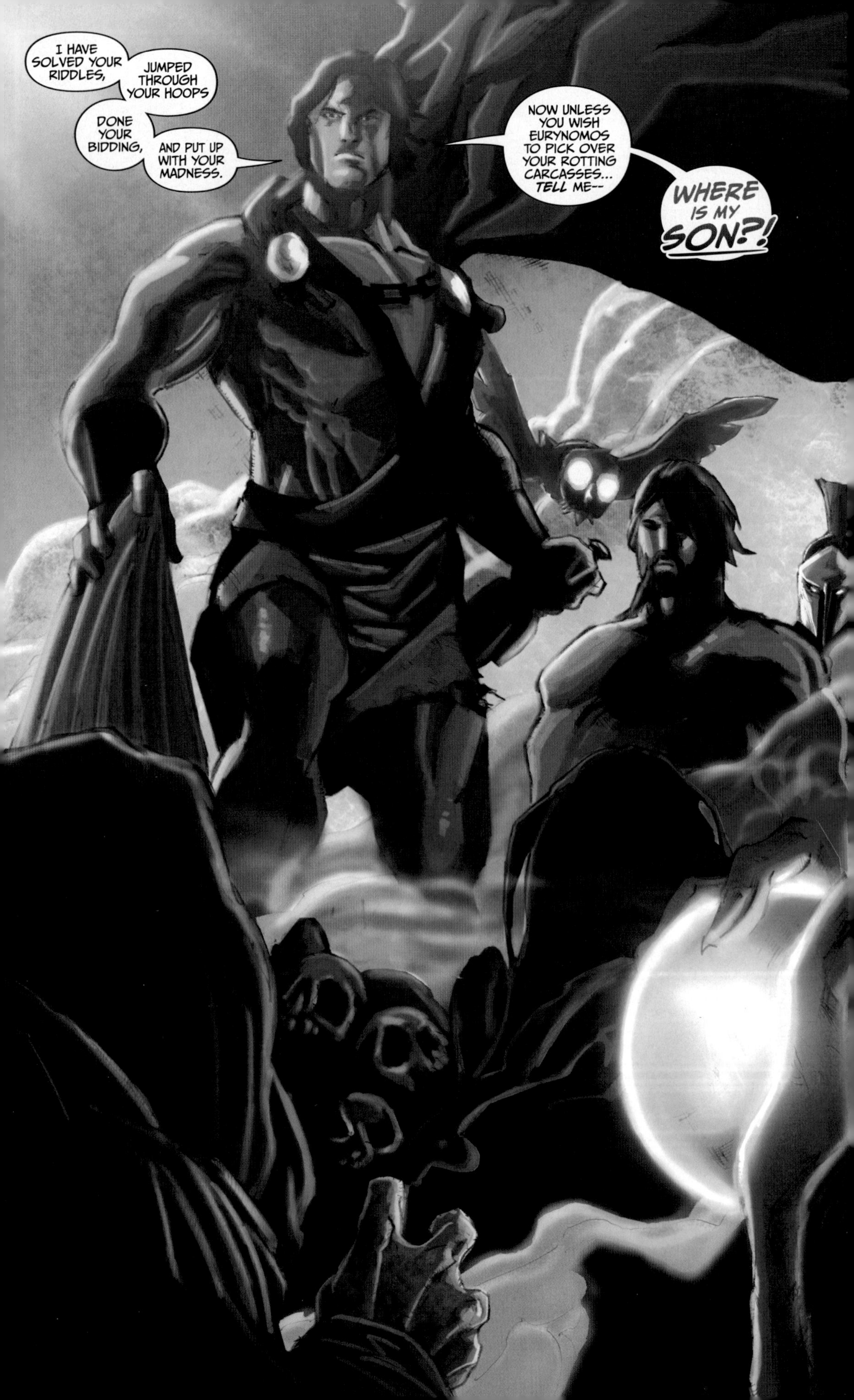
I HAVE SOLVED YOUR RIDDLES,
JUMPED THROUGH YOUR HOOPS
DONE YOUR BIDDING,
AND PUT UP WITH YOUR MADNESS.
NOW UNLESS YOU WISH EURYNOMOS TO PICK OVER YOUR ROTTING CARCASSES... TELL ME--
WHERE IS MY SON?!

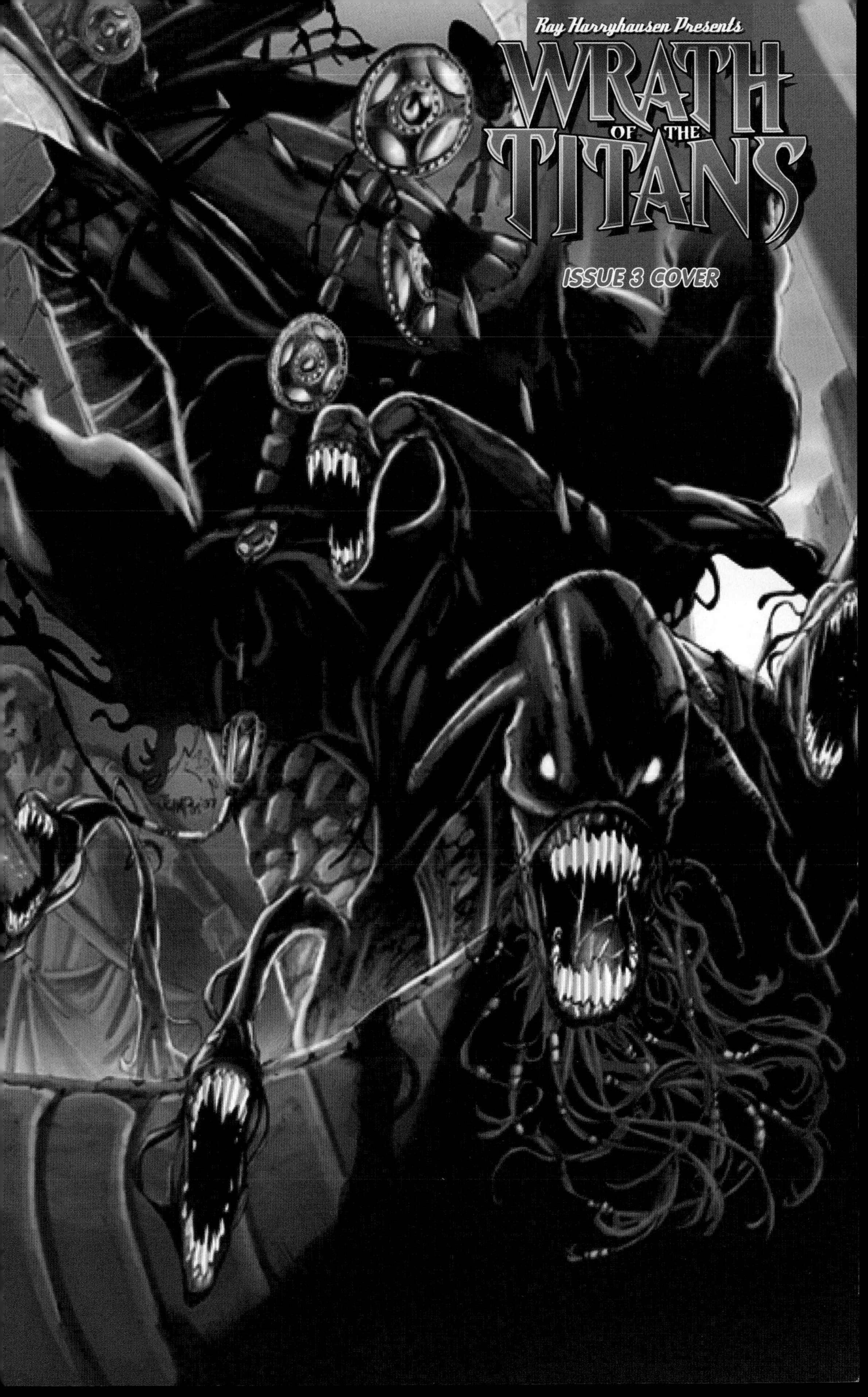
Ray Harryhausen Presents
WRATH OF THE TITANS
ISSUE 3 COVER

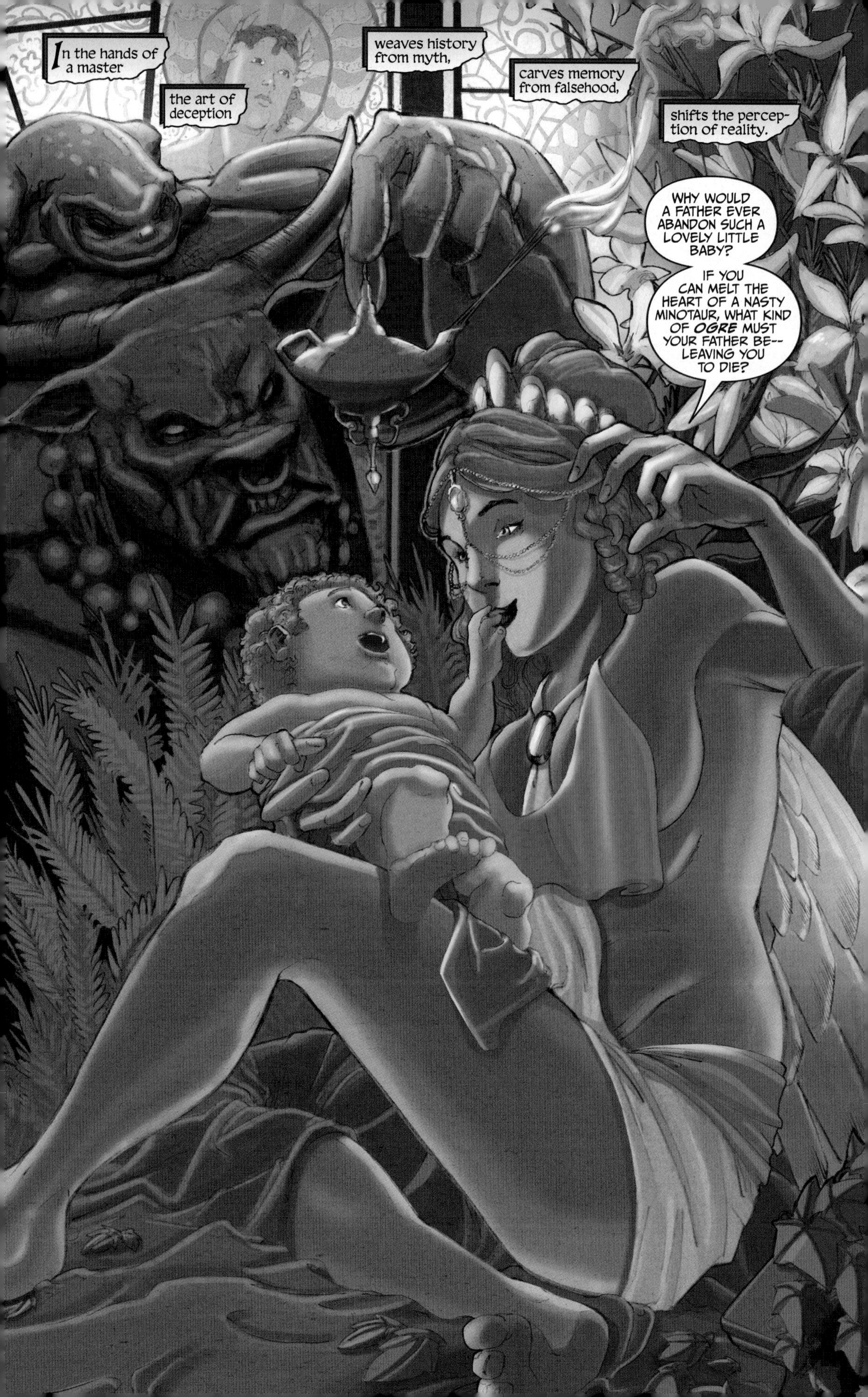
In the hands of a master
the art of deception
weaves history from myth,
carves memory from falsehood,
shifts the perception of reality.
WHY WOULD A FATHER EVER ABANDON SUCH A LOVELY LITTLE BABY?
IF YOU CAN MELT THE HEART OF A NASTY MINOTAUR, WHAT KIND OF OGRE MUST YOUR FATHER BE--LEAVING YOU TO DIE?

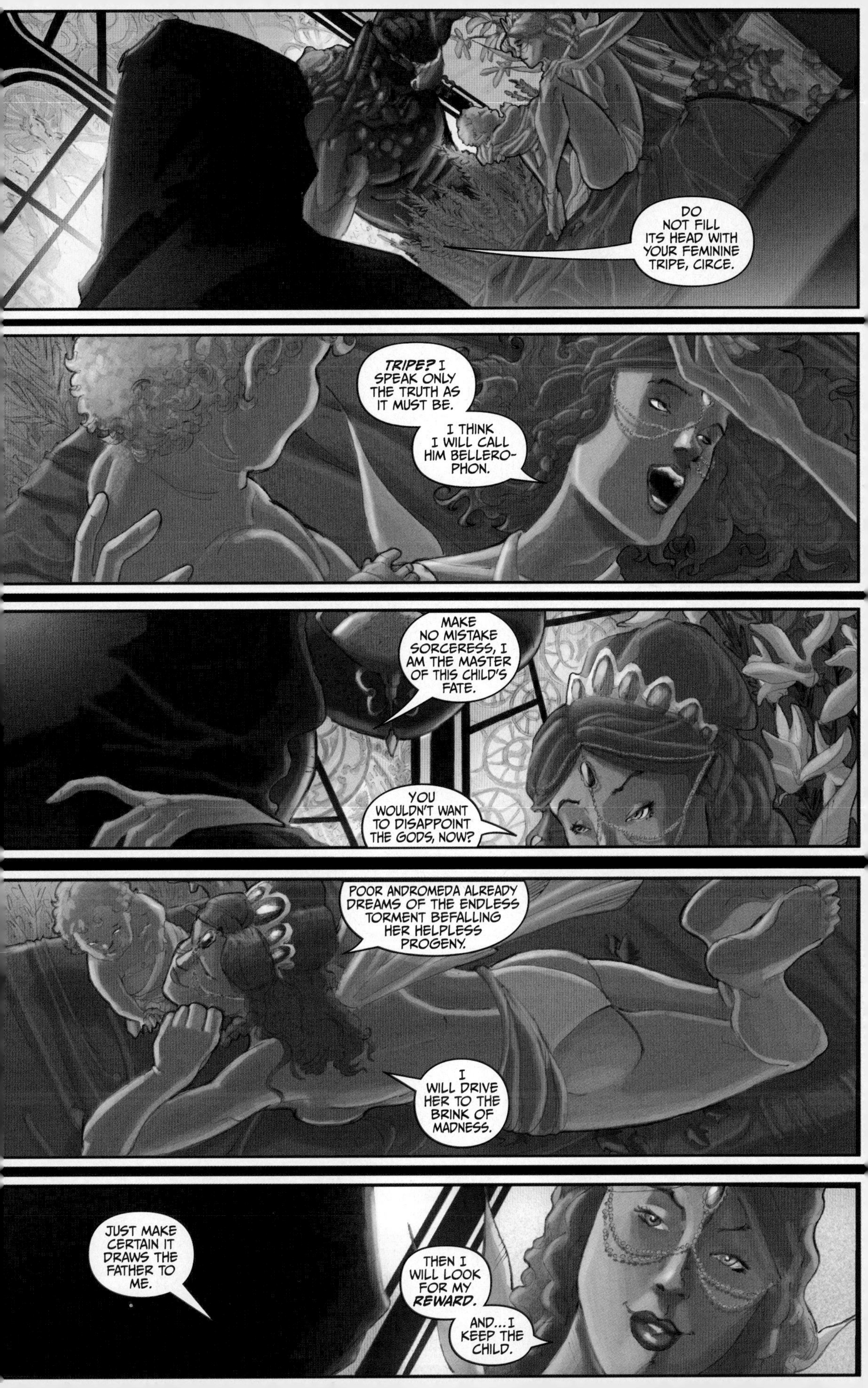
DO NOT FILL ITS HEAD WITH YOUR FEMININE TRIPE, CIRCE.
TRIPE? I SPEAK ONLY THE TRUTH AS IT MUST BE.
I THINK I WILL CALL HIM BELLEROPHON.
MAKE NO MISTAKE SORCERESS, I AM THE MASTER OF THIS CHILD'S FATE.
YOU WOULDN'T WANT TO DISAPPOINT THE GODS, NOW?
POOR ANDROMEDA ALREADY DREAMS OF THE ENDLESS TORMENT BEFALLING HER HELPLESS PROGENY.
I WILL DRIVE HER TO THE BRINK OF MADNESS.
JUST MAKE CERTAIN IT DRAWS THE FATHER TO ME.
THEN I WILL LOOK FOR MY ***REWARD.***
AND...I KEEP THE CHILD.

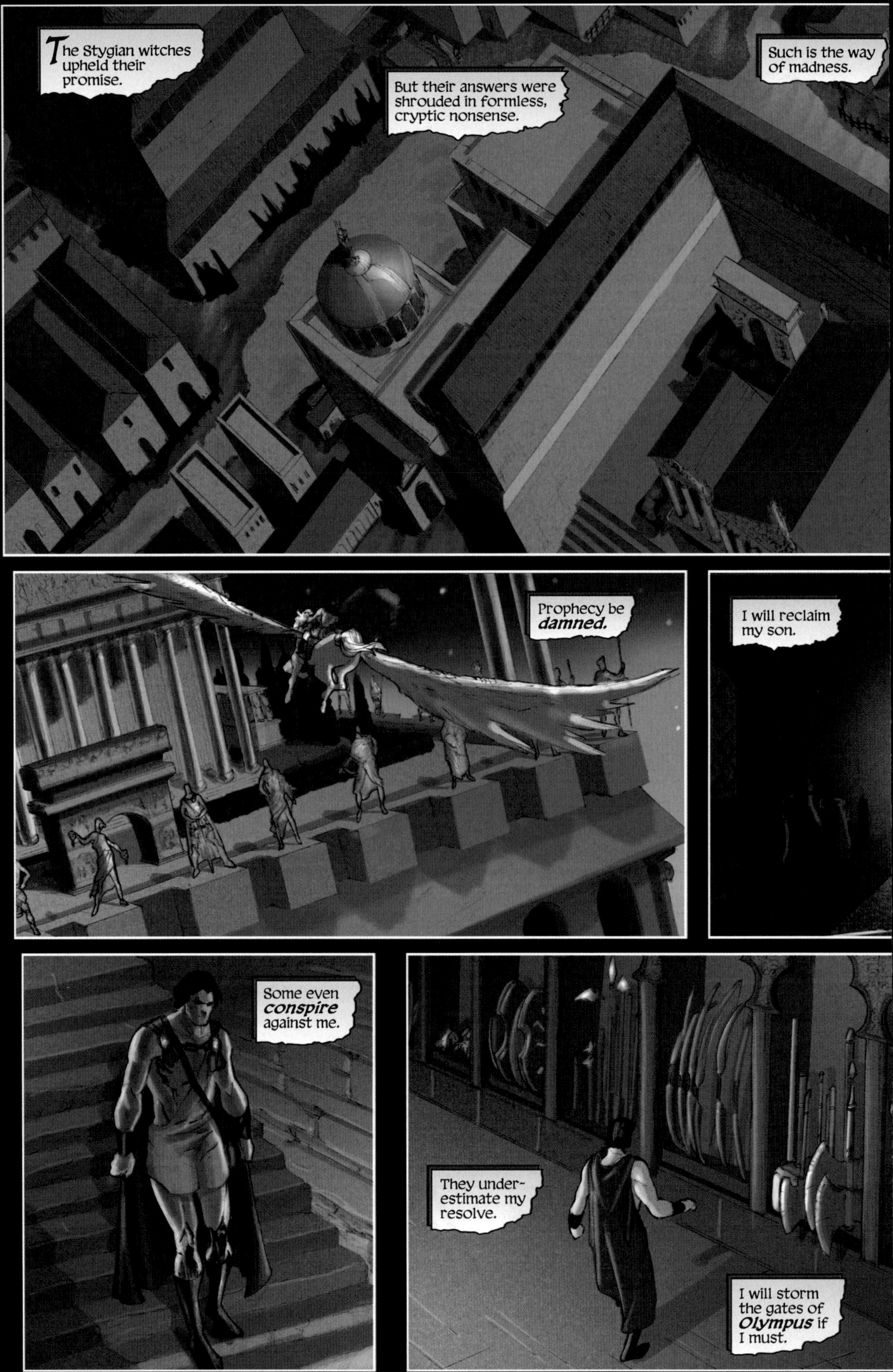
The Stygian witches upheld their promise.
But their answers were shrouded in formless, cryptic nonsense.
Such is the way of madness.
Prophecy be *damned.*
I will reclaim my son.
Some even *conspire* against me.
They under-estimate my resolve.
I will storm the gates of *Olympus* if I must.

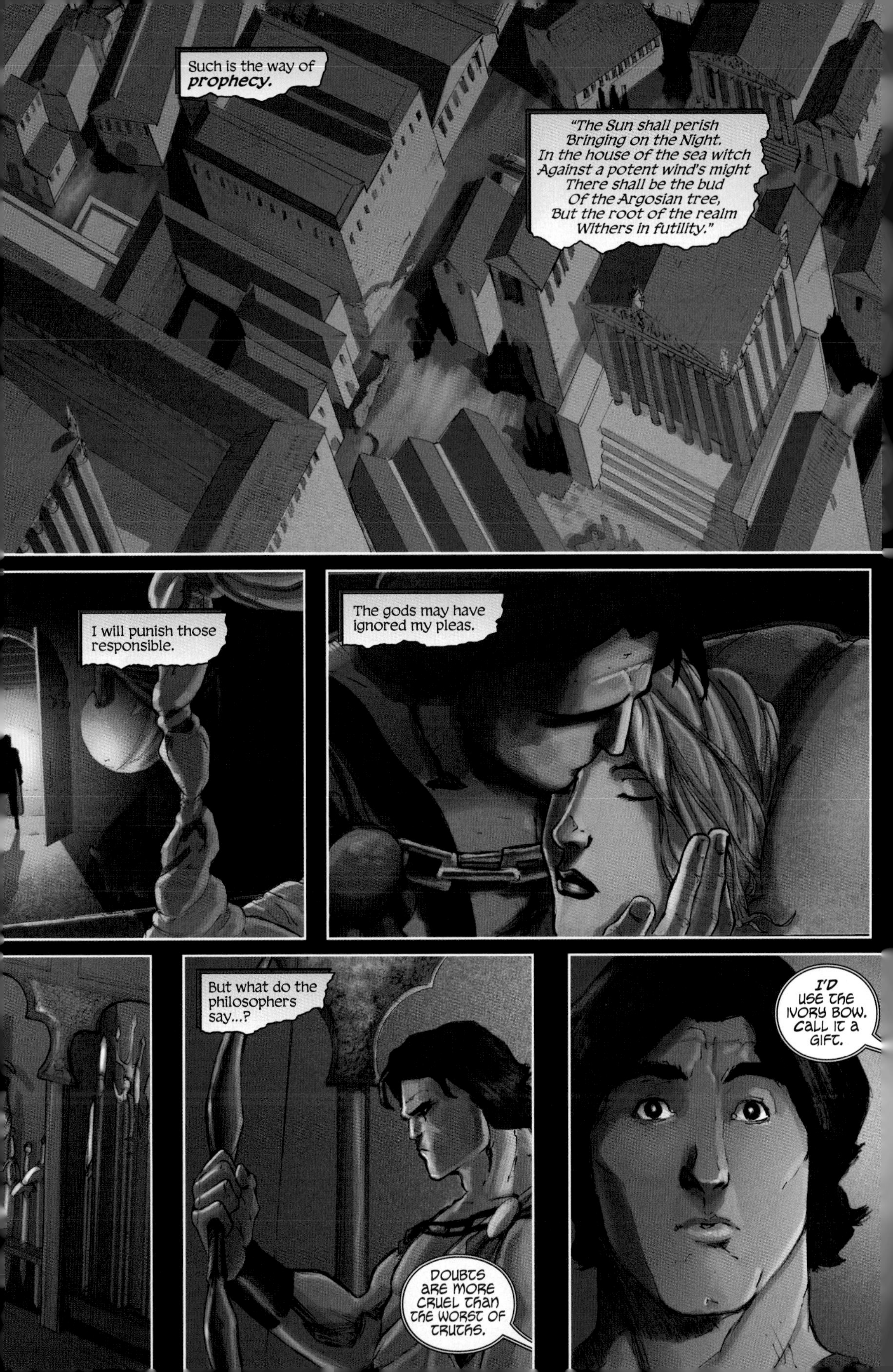
Such is the way of **prophecy.**
"The Sun shall perish Bringing on the Night. In the house of the sea witch Against a potent wind's might There shall be the bud Of the Argosian tree, But the root of the realm Withers in futility."
I will punish those responsible.
The gods may have ignored my pleas.
But what do the philosophers say...?
DOUBTS ARE MORE CRUEL THAN THE WORST OF TRUTHS.
I'D USE THE IVORY BOW. CALL IT A GIFT.

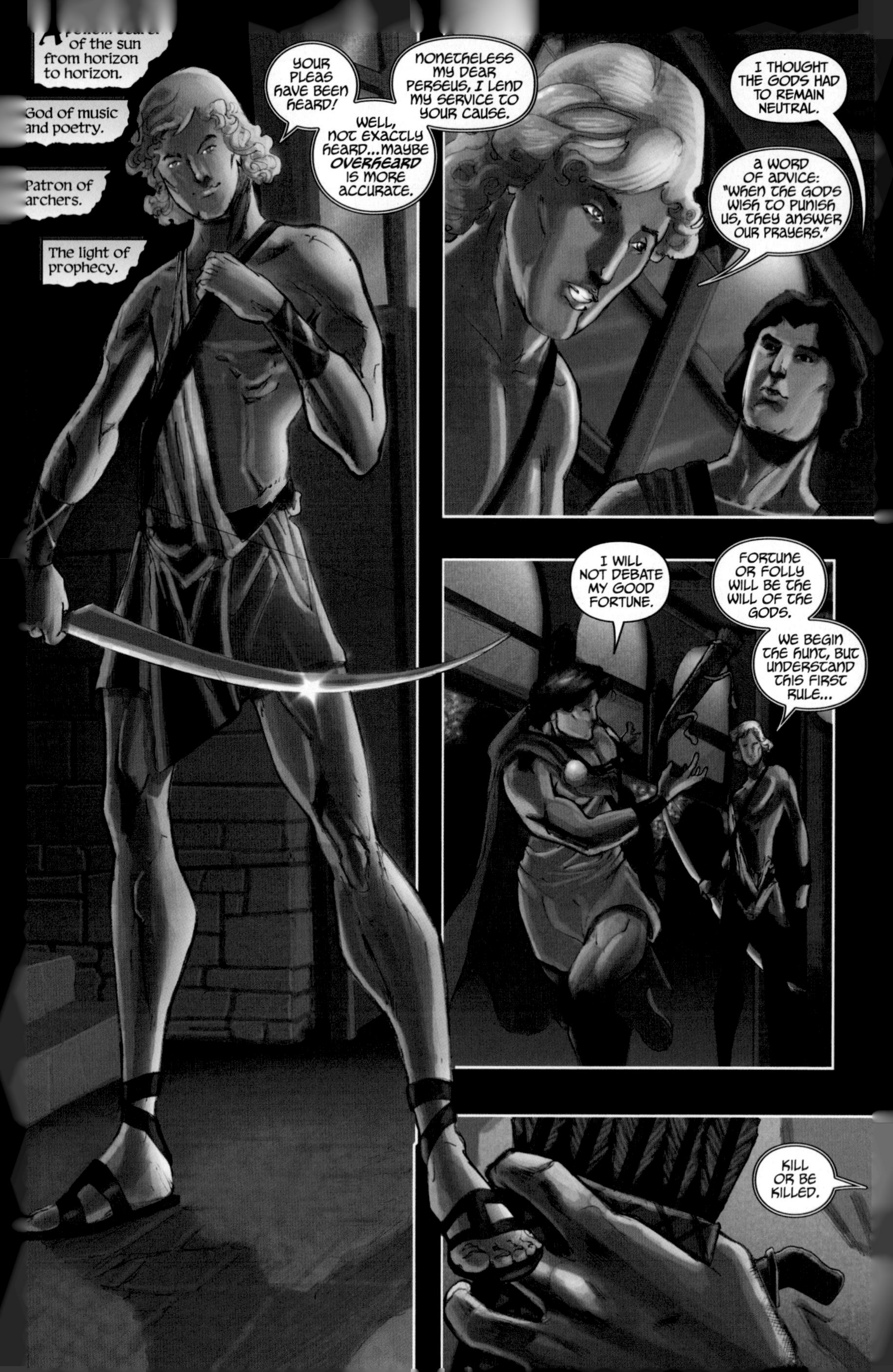

of the sun from horizon to horizon.
God of music and poetry.
Patron of archers.
The light of prophecy.
YOUR PLEAS HAVE BEEN HEARD!
NONETHELESS MY DEAR PERSEUS, I LEND MY SERVICE TO YOUR CAUSE.
WELL, NOT EXACTLY HEARD...MAYBE OVERHEARD IS MORE ACCURATE.
I THOUGHT THE GODS HAD TO REMAIN NEUTRAL.
A WORD OF ADVICE: "WHEN THE GODS WISH TO PUNISH US, THEY ANSWER OUR PRAYERS."
I WILL NOT DEBATE MY GOOD FORTUNE.
FORTUNE OR FOLLY WILL BE THE WILL OF THE GODS.
WE BEGIN THE HUNT, BUT UNDERSTAND THIS FIRST RULE...
KILL OR BE KILLED.

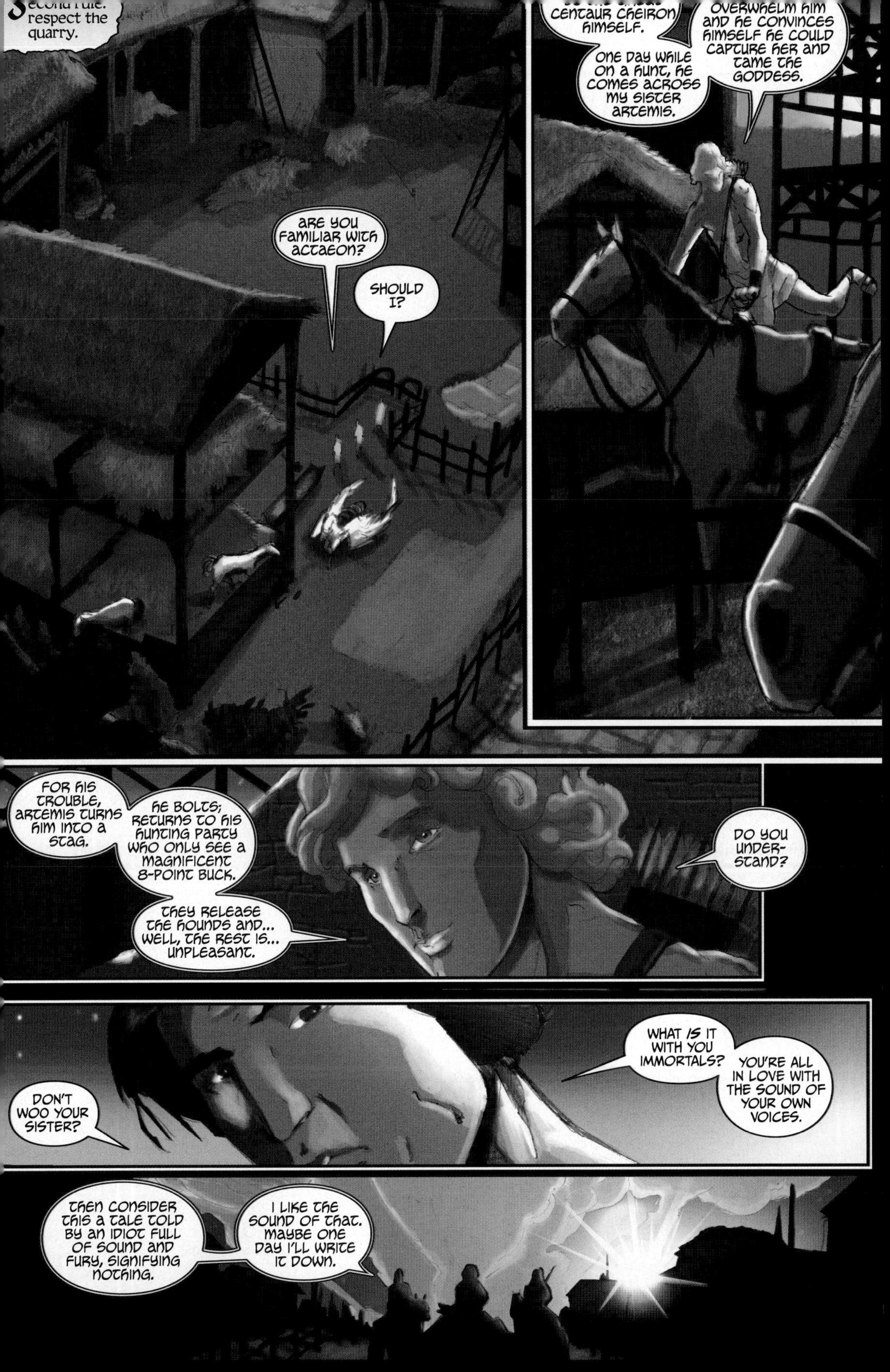
Second rule: respect the quarry.
ARE YOU FAMILIAR WITH ACTAEON?
SHOULD I?
CENTAUR CHEIRON HIMSELF.
ONE DAY WHILE ON A HUNT, HE COMES ACROSS MY SISTER ARTEMIS.
OVERWHELM HIM AND HE CONVINCES HIMSELF HE COULD CAPTURE HER AND TAME THE GODDESS.
FOR HIS TROUBLE, ARTEMIS TURNS HIM INTO A STAG.
HE BOLTS; RETURNS TO HIS HUNTING PARTY WHO ONLY SEE A MAGNIFICENT 8-POINT BUCK.
THEY RELEASE THE HOUNDS AND... WELL, THE REST IS... UNPLEASANT.
DO YOU UNDER-STAND?
DON'T WOO YOUR SISTER?
WHAT *IS* IT WITH YOU IMMORTALS?
YOU'RE ALL IN LOVE WITH THE SOUND OF YOUR OWN VOICES.
THEN CONSIDER THIS A TALE TOLD BY AN IDIOT FULL OF SOUND AND FURY, SIGNIFYING NOTHING.
I LIKE THE SOUND OF THAT. MAYBE ONE DAY I'LL WRITE IT DOWN.

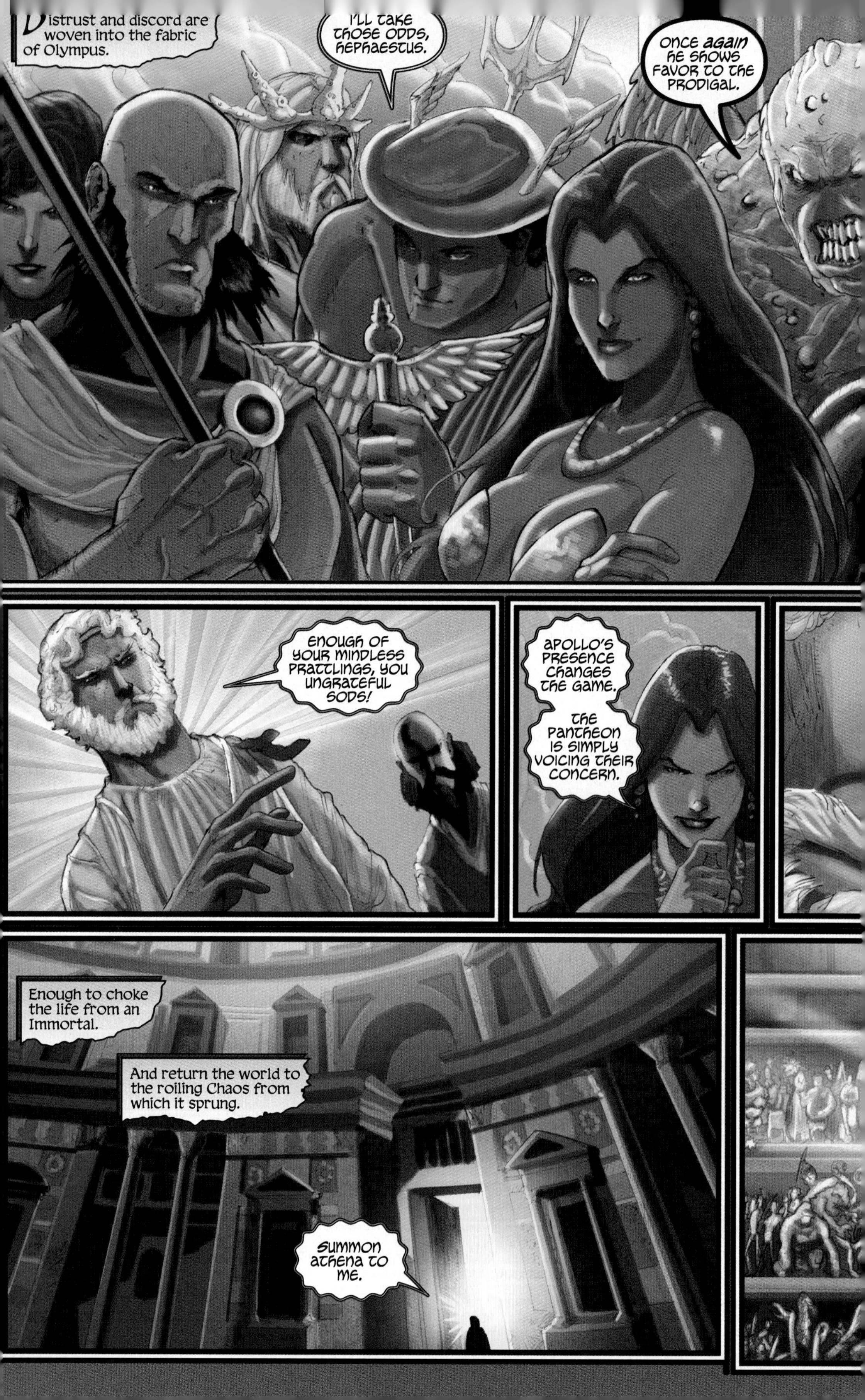
Distrust and discord are woven into the fabric of Olympus.
I'LL TAKE THOSE ODDS, HEPHAESTUS.
ONCE AGAIN HE SHOWS FAVOR TO THE PRODIGAL.
ENOUGH OF YOUR MINDLESS PRATTLINGS, YOU UNGRATEFUL SODS!
APOLLO'S PRESENCE CHANGES THE GAME.
THE PANTHEON IS SIMPLY VOICING THEIR CONCERN.
Enough to choke the life from an Immortal.
And return the world to the roiling Chaos from which it sprung.
SUMMON ATHENA TO ME.

HADES IS RIGHT. ZEUS CANNOT BE TRUSTED.

FAVOR OR NONE, THIS TIME THE MIGHTY PERSEUS WILL FALL.

APOLLO MUST BE THWARTED.

THIS PURGE SHOULD NOT STOP WITH APOLLO.

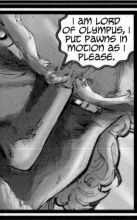

I AM LORD OF OLYMPUS, I PUT PAWNS IN MOTION AS I PLEASE.

PAWNS ARE THE FIRST TO BE SACRIFICED IN WAR, HUSBAND.

EVEN PRIZED PAWNS.

And all too often the knots and loose threads of intrigue form a *noose*.

I DID NOT ANTICIPATE APOLLO'S FOLLY. THIS COMPLICATES MATTERS.

THERE IS A WAY WE CAN KEEP HIM IN CHECK, FATHER.

Artemis. Apollo's twin. Goddess of the hunt.

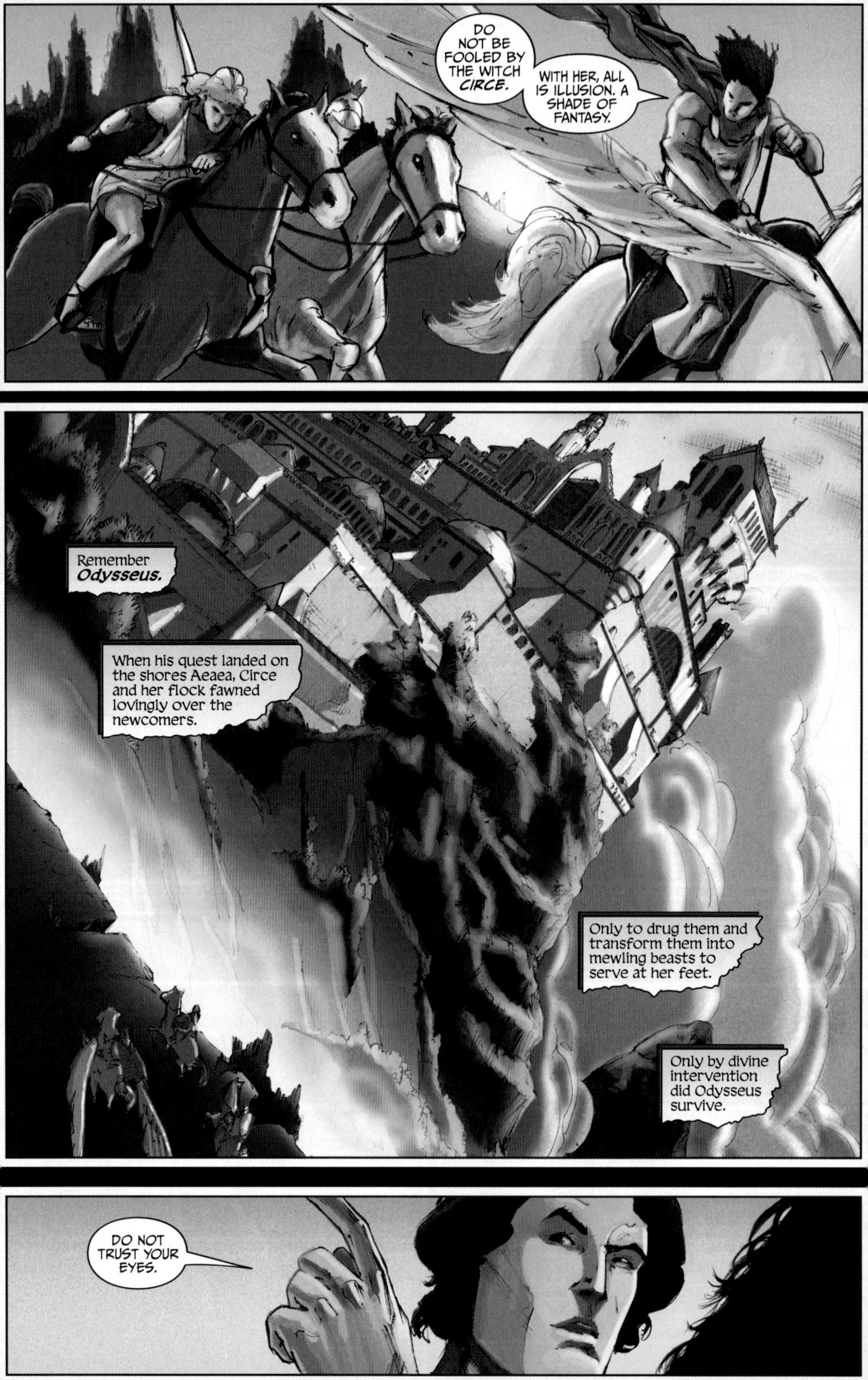
DO NOT BE FOOLED BY THE WITCH CIRCE.
WITH HER, ALL IS ILLUSION. A SHADE OF FANTASY.
Remember Odysseus.
When his quest landed on the shores Aeaea, Circe and her flock fawned lovingly over the newcomers.
Only to drug them and transform them into mewling beasts to serve at her feet.
Only by divine intervention did Odysseus survive.
DO NOT TRUST YOUR EYES.

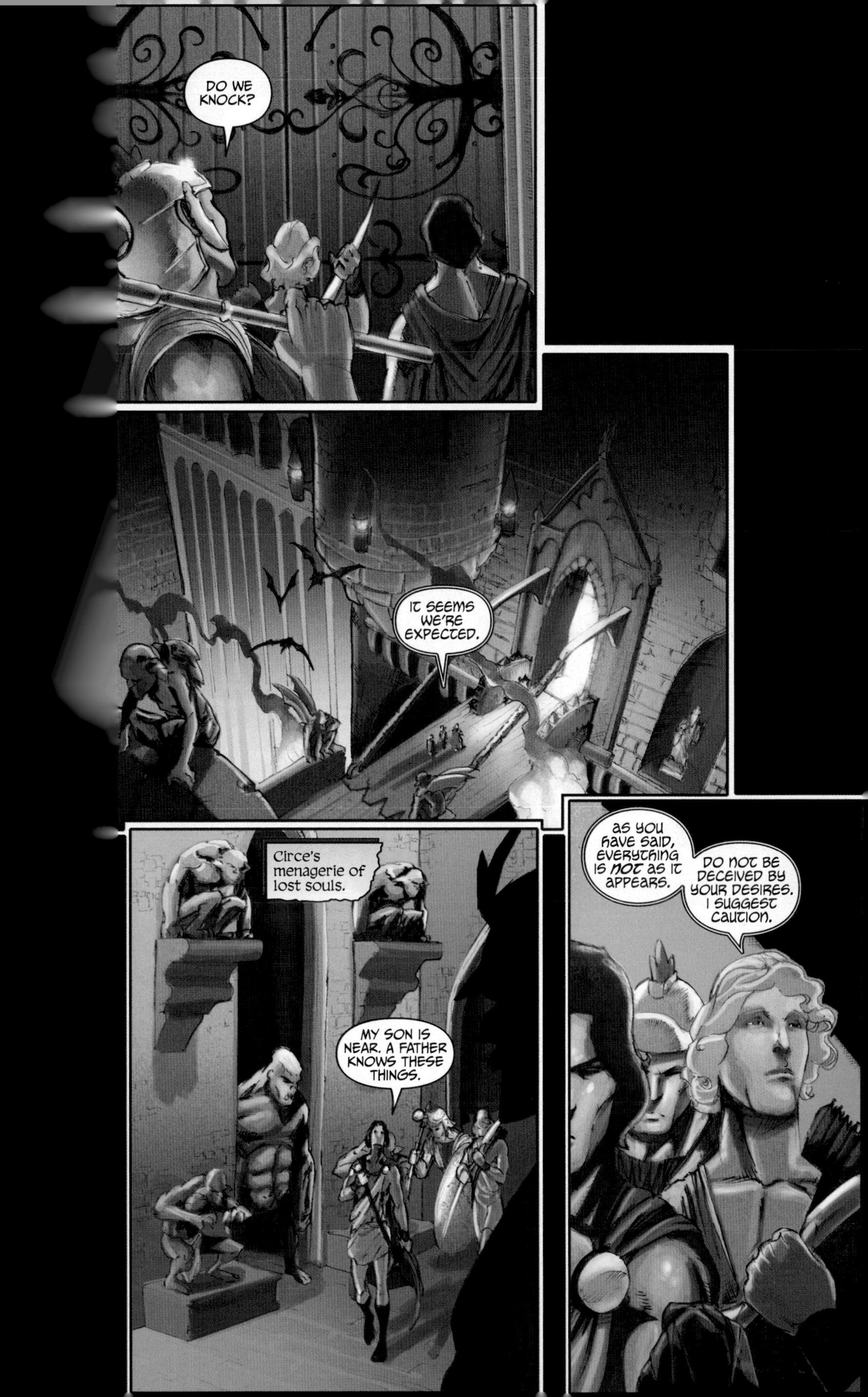
DO WE KNOCK?
IT SEEMS WE'RE EXPECTED.
Circe's menagerie of lost souls.
MY SON IS NEAR. A FATHER KNOWS THESE THINGS.
AS YOU HAVE SAID, EVERYTHING IS *NOT* AS IT APPEARS.
DO NOT BE DECEIVED BY YOUR DESIRES. I SUGGEST CAUTION.

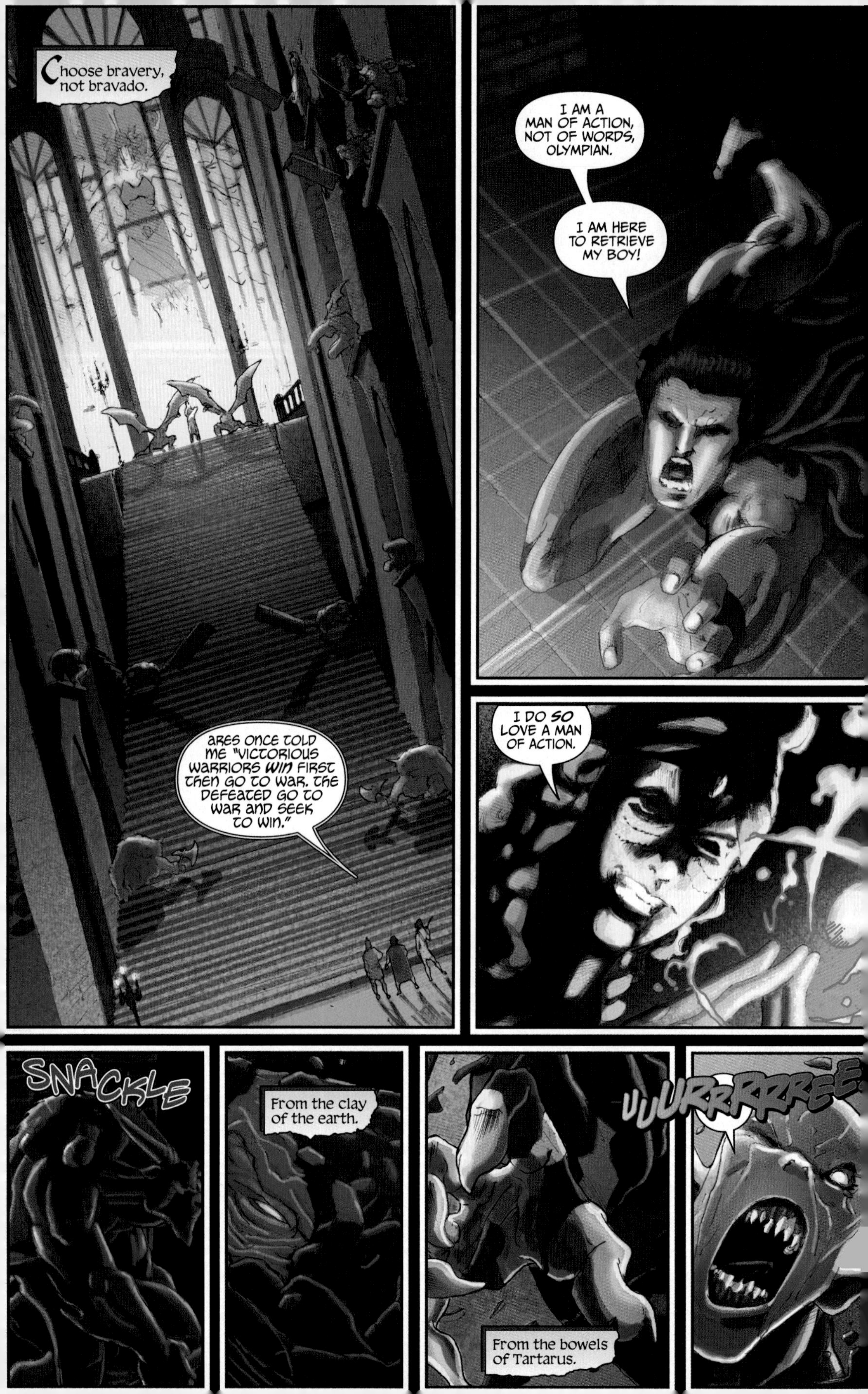
Choose bravery, not bravado.
ARES ONCE TOLD ME "VICTORIOUS WARRIORS WIN FIRST THEN GO TO WAR. THE DEFEATED GO TO WAR AND SEEK TO WIN."
I AM A MAN OF ACTION, NOT OF WORDS, OLYMPIAN.
I AM HERE TO RETRIEVE MY BOY!
I DO SO LOVE A MAN OF ACTION.
SNACKLE
From the clay of the earth.
From the bowels of Tartarus.
UUURRRRREE

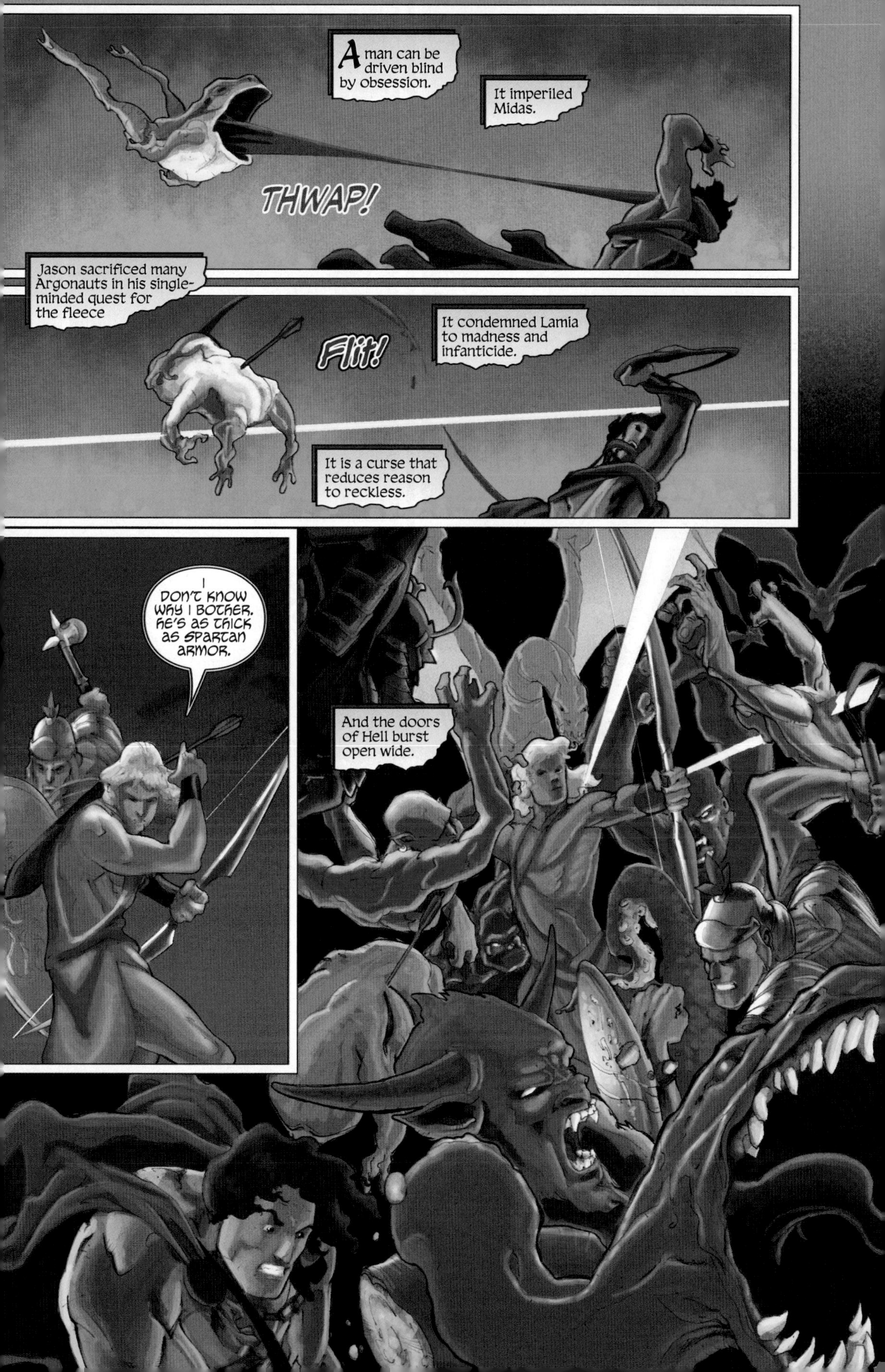
A man can be driven blind by obsession.
It imperiled Midas.
THWAP!
Jason sacrificed many Argonauts in his single-minded quest for the fleece
Flit!
It condemned Lamia to madness and infanticide.
It is a curse that reduces reason to reckless.
I DON'T KNOW WHY I BOTHER. HE'S AS THICK AS SPARTAN ARMOR.
And the doors of Hell burst open wide.

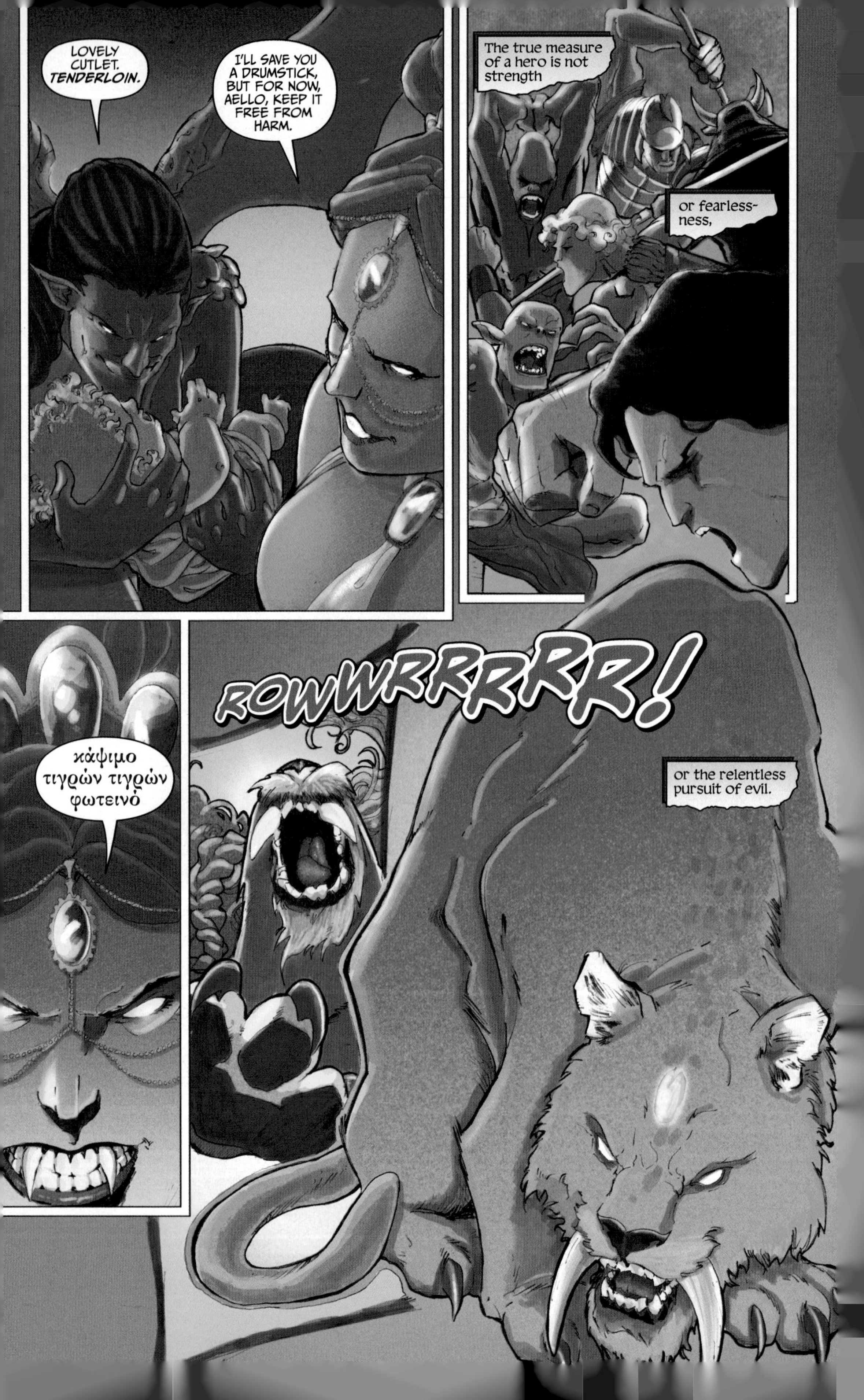
LOVELY CUTLET. TENDERLOIN.
I'LL SAVE YOU A DRUMSTICK, BUT FOR NOW, AELLO, KEEP IT FREE FROM HARM.
The true measure of a hero is not strength
or fearless-ness,
κάψιμο τιγρών τιγρών φωτεινό
ROWWRRRRR!
or the relentless pursuit of evil.

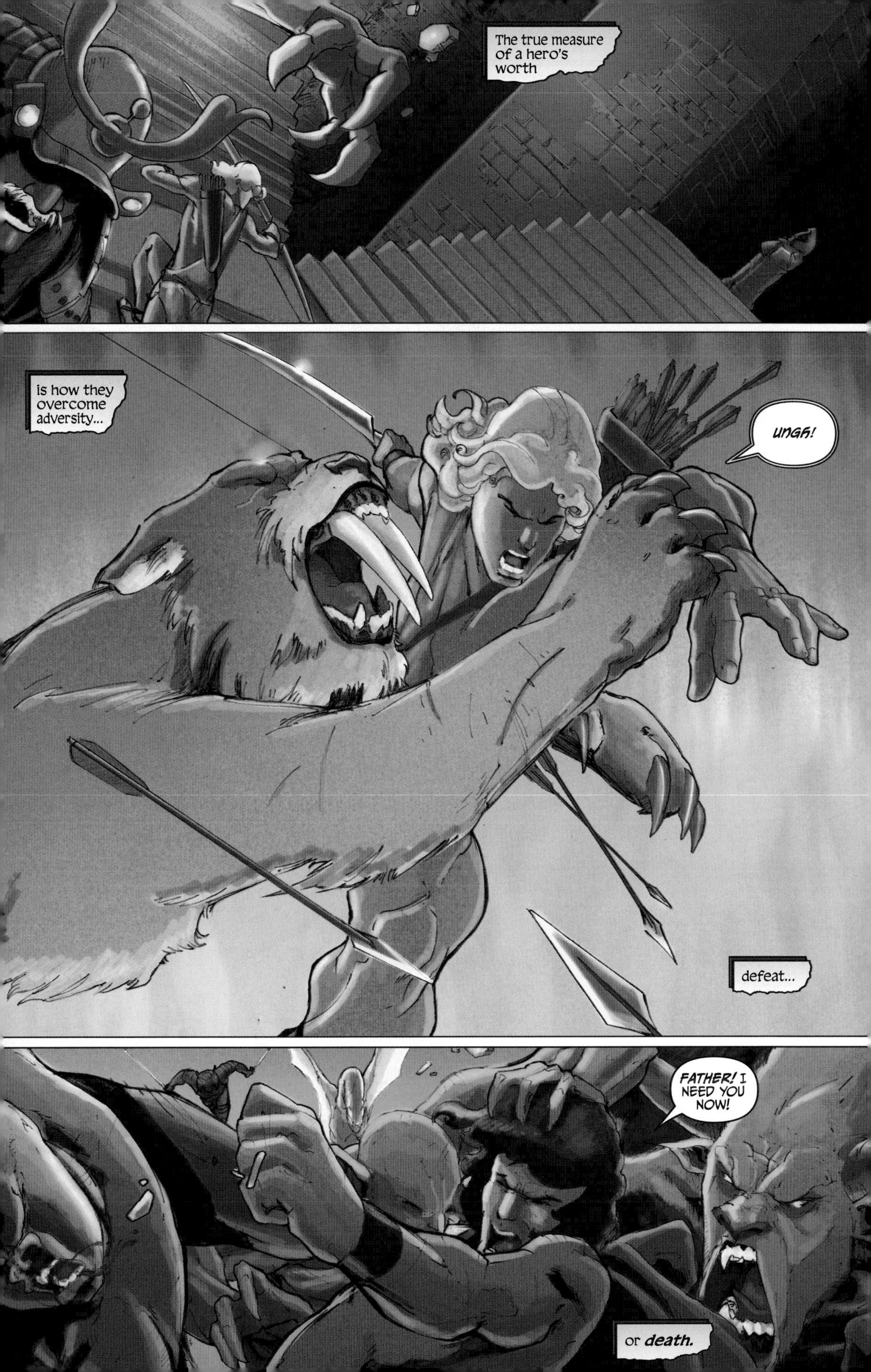
The true measure of a hero's worth
is how they overcome adversity...
UNGH!
defeat...
FATHER! I NEED YOU NOW!
or *death.*

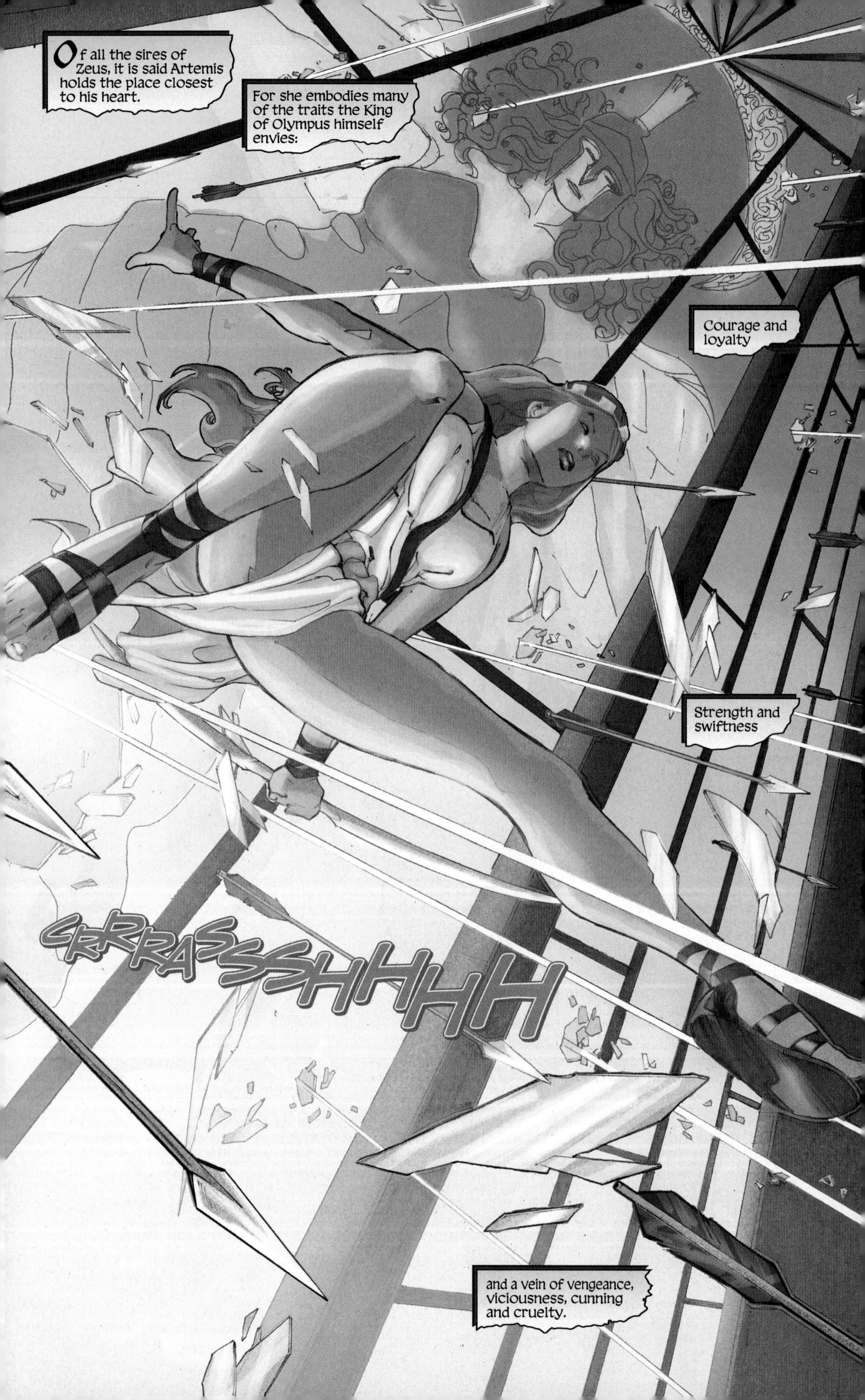
Of all the sires of Zeus, it is said Artemis holds the place closest to his heart.
For she embodies many of the traits the King of Olympus himself envies:
Courage and loyalty
Strength and swiftness
CRRRASSSHHHHH
and a vein of vengeance, viciousness, cunning and cruelty.

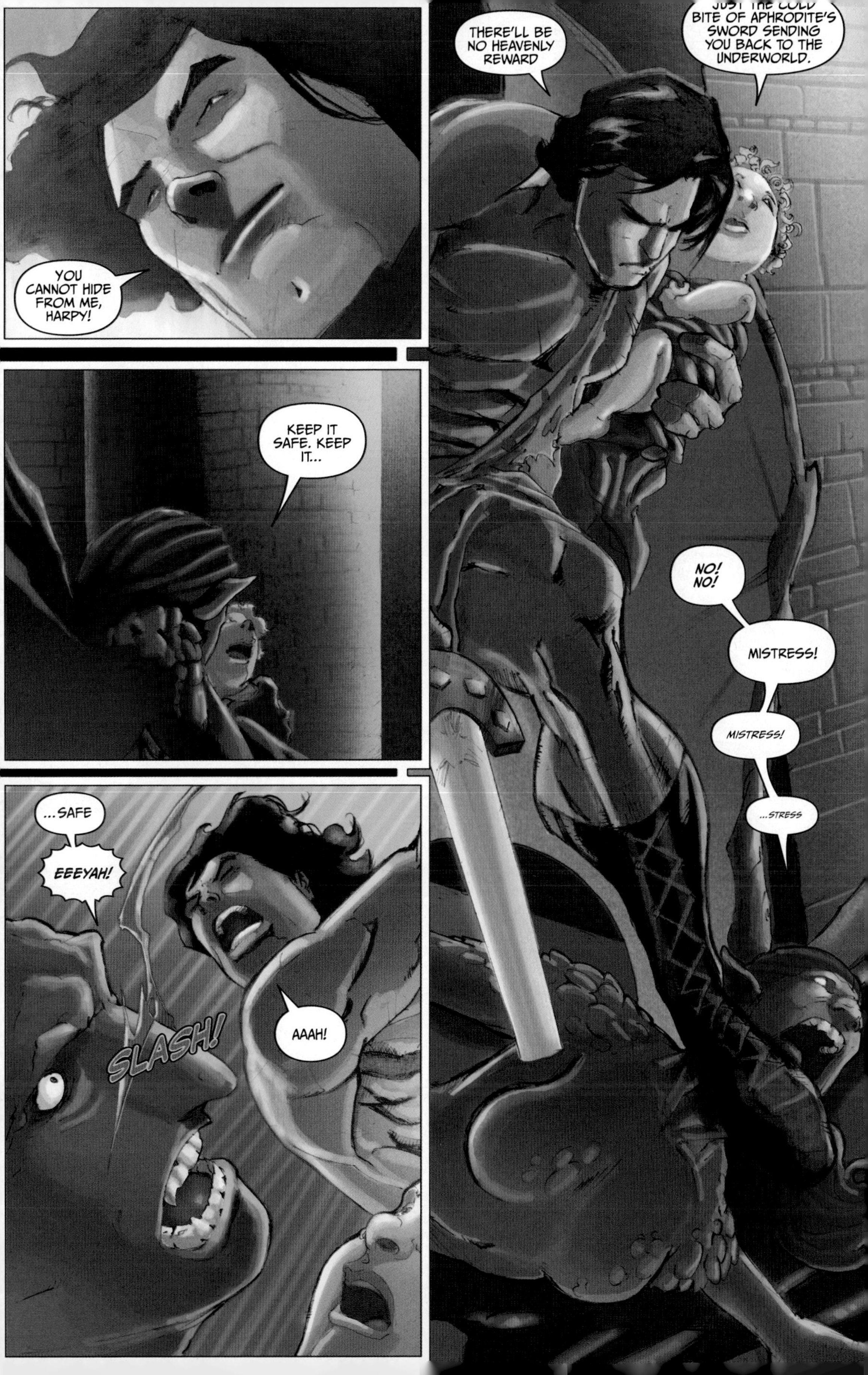
YOU CANNOT HIDE FROM ME, HARPY!
KEEP IT SAFE. KEEP IT...
...SAFE
EEEYAH!
SLASH!
AAAH!
THERE'LL BE NO HEAVENLY REWARD
JUST THE COLD BITE OF APHRODITE'S SWORD SENDING YOU BACK TO THE UNDERWORLD.
NO! NO!
MISTRESS!
MISTRESS!
...STRESS

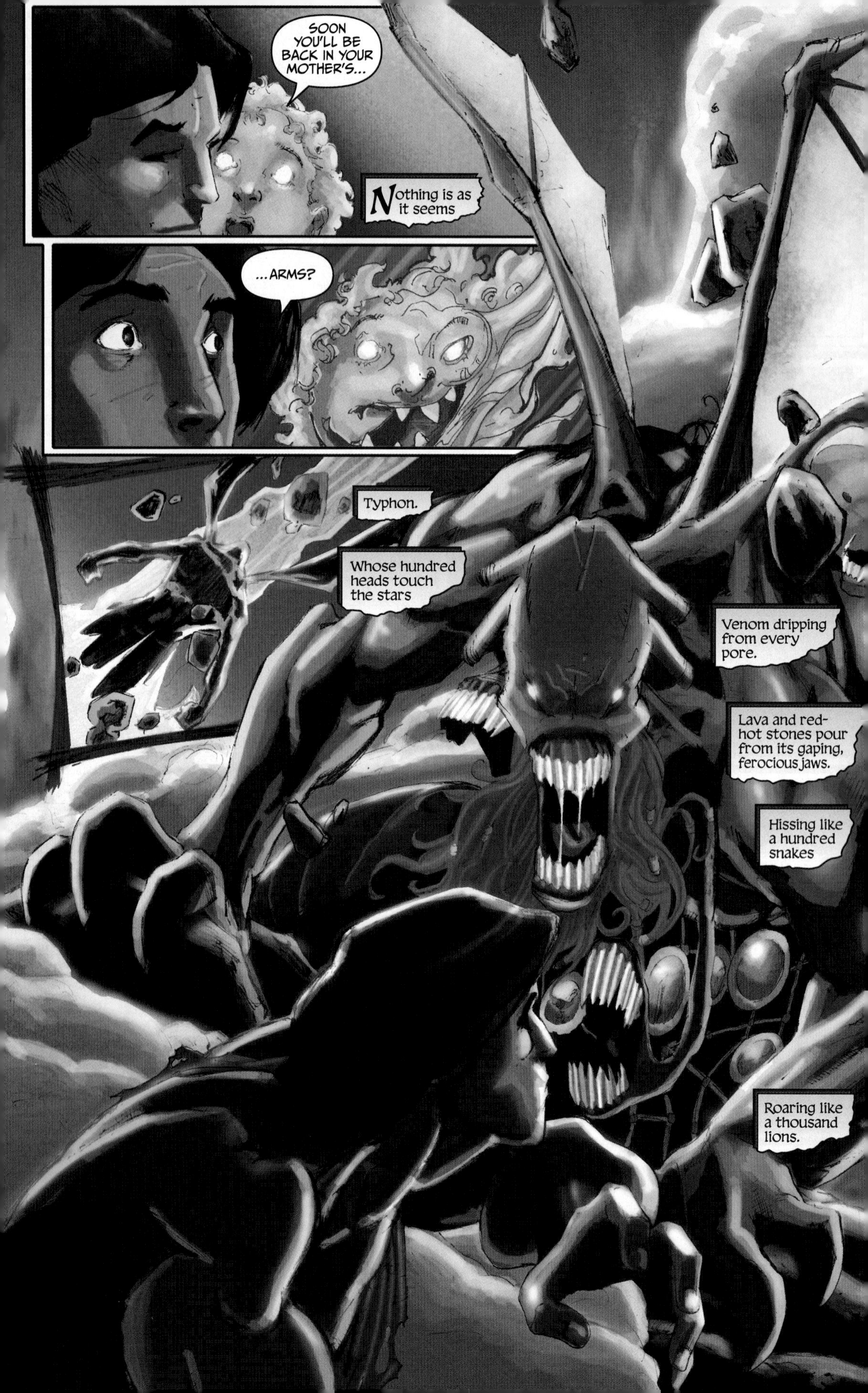
SOON YOU'LL BE BACK IN YOUR MOTHER'S...
Nothing is as it seems
...ARMS?
Typhon.
Whose hundred heads touch the stars
Venom dripping from every pore.
Lava and red-hot stones pour from its gaping, ferocious jaws.
Hissing like a hundred snakes
Roaring like a thousand lions.

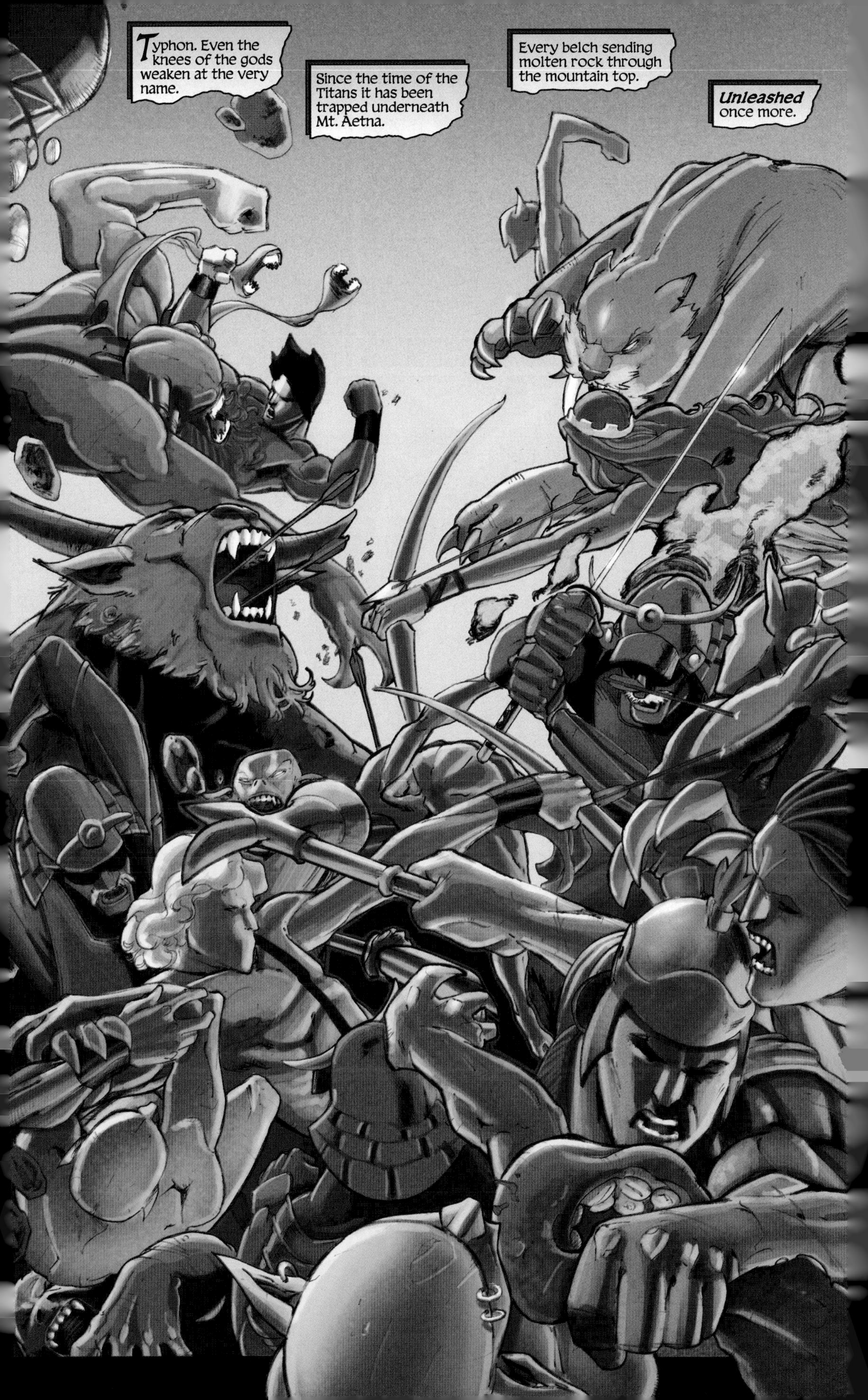
Typhon. Even the knees of the gods weaken at the very name.
Since the time of the Titans it has been trapped underneath Mt. Aetna.
Every belch sending molten rock through the mountain top.
Unleashed once more.

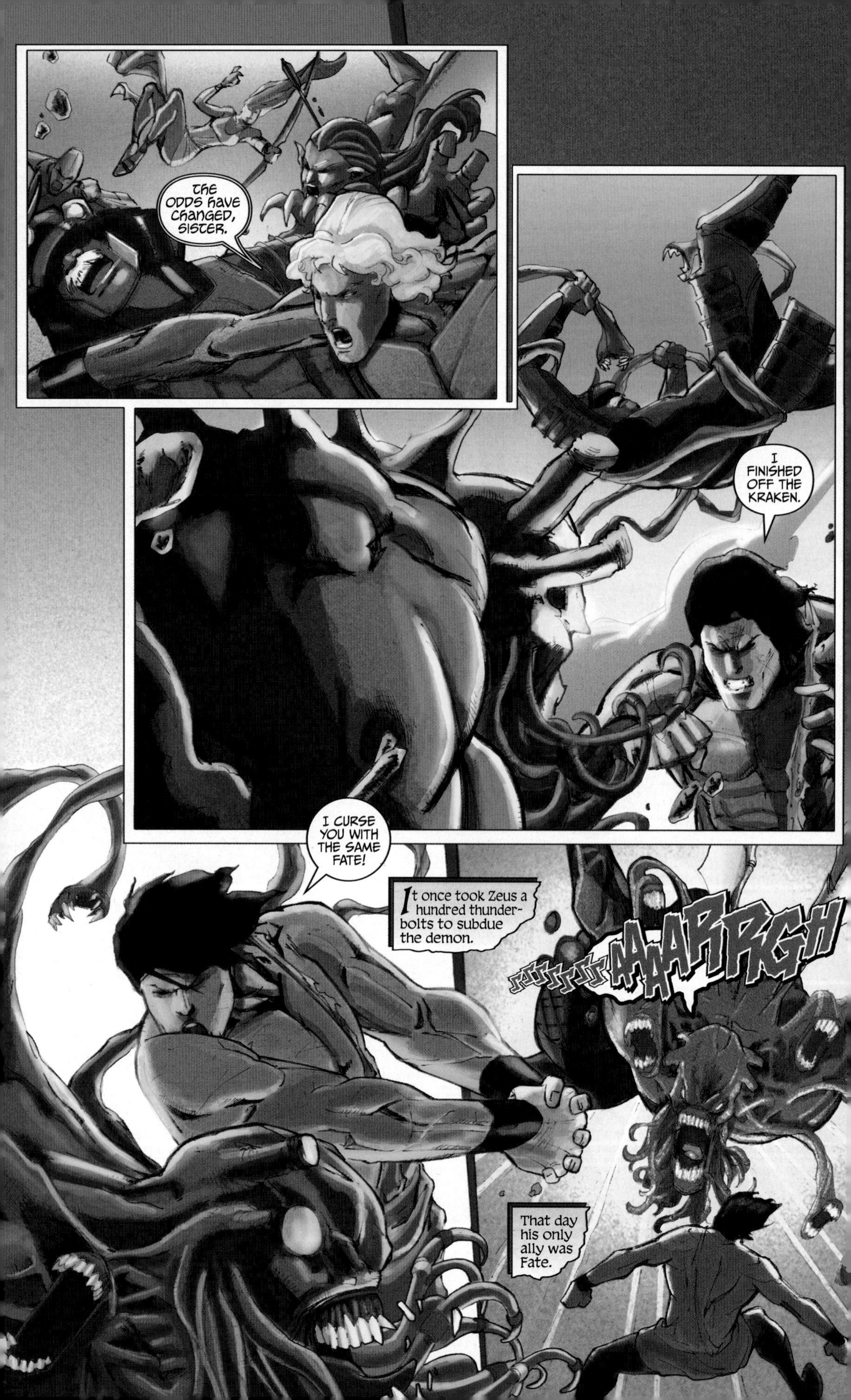

THE ODDS HAVE CHANGED, SISTER.
I FINISHED OFF THE KRAKEN.
I CURSE YOU WITH THE SAME FATE!
It once took Zeus a hundred thunder-bolts to subdue the demon.
That day his only ally was Fate.

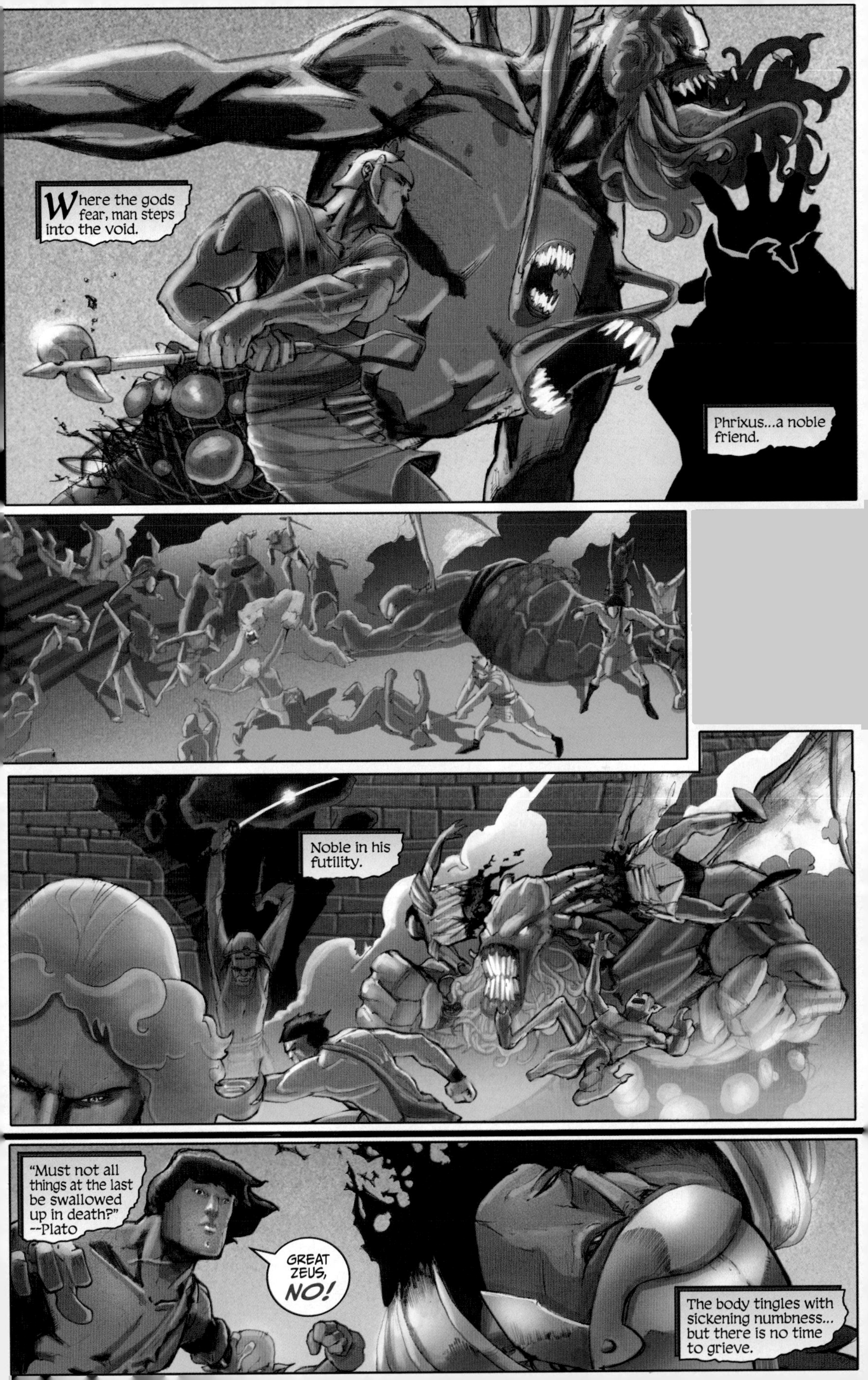
Where the gods fear, man steps into the void.
Phrixus...a noble friend.
Noble in his futility.
"Must not all things at the last be swallowed up in death?" --Plato
GREAT ZEUS, NO!
The body tingles with sickening numbness... but there is no time to grieve.

I am nothing but a straw doll...

SLASH

YAH!

Stuck knee-deep in the silt of the Aegean...and the tide is rising.

SO CIRCE LET YOU OUT OF YOUR CAGE.

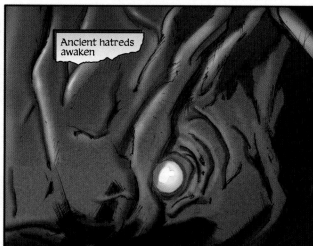

Ancient hatreds awaken

ARTEMIS! FEEL MY WRATH!

That not even the gods can contain.

KRRAAK

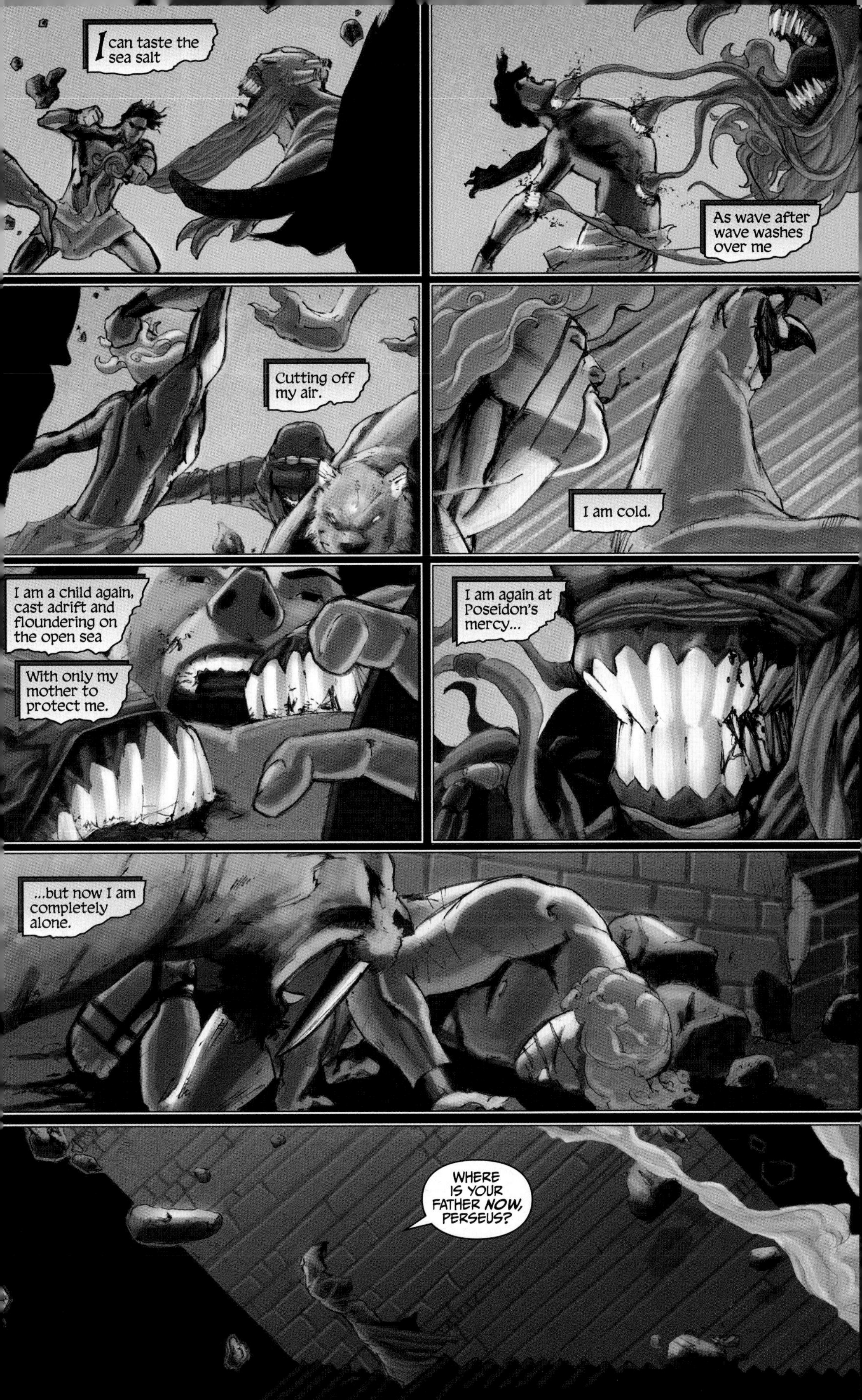
I can taste the sea salt
As wave after wave washes over me
Cutting off my air.
I am cold.
I am a child again, cast adrift and floundering on the open sea
With only my mother to protect me.
I am again at Poseidon's mercy...
...but now I am completely alone.
WHERE IS YOUR FATHER NOW, PERSEUS?

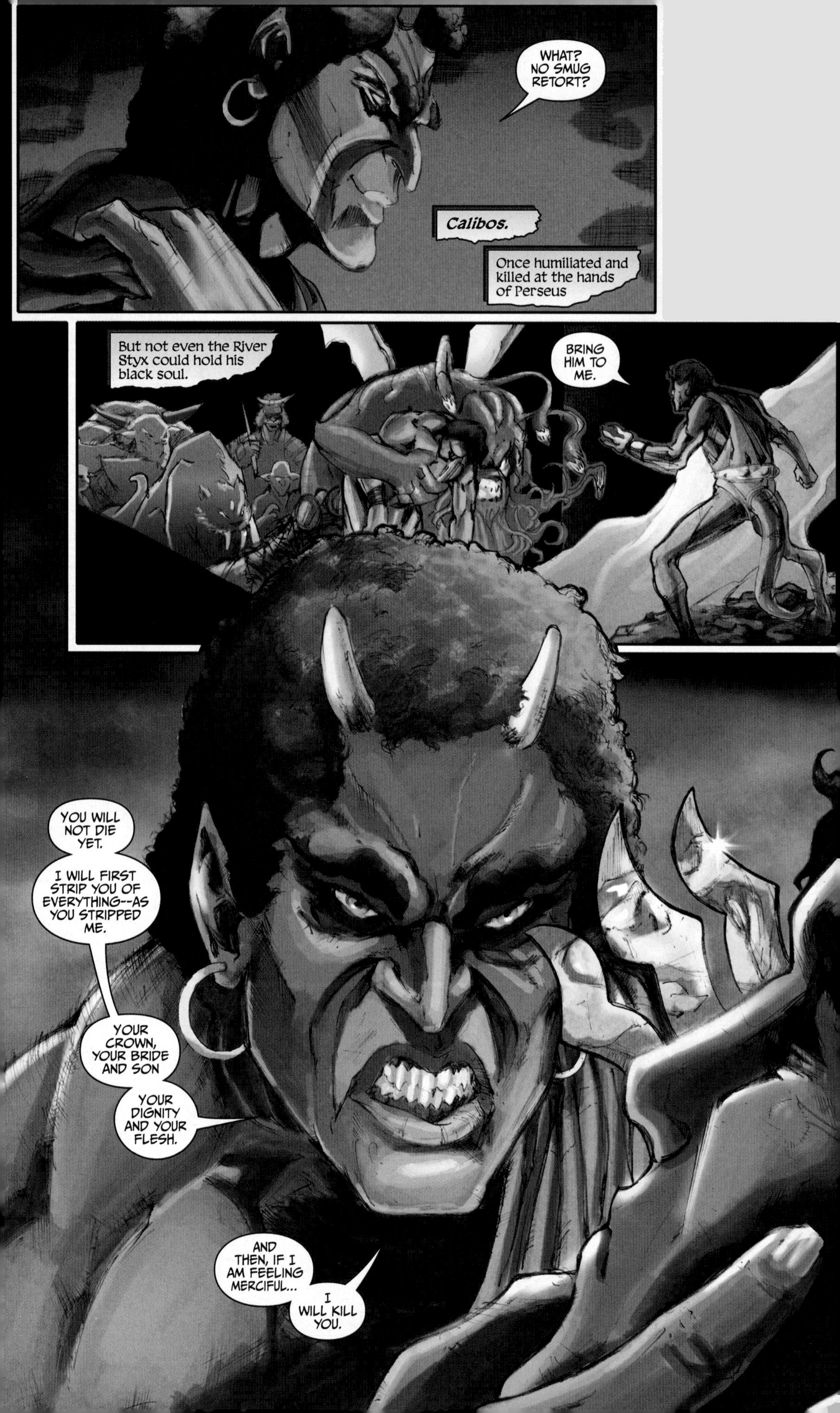
WHAT? NO SMUG RETORT?
Calibos.
Once humiliated and killed at the hands of Perseus
But not even the River Styx could hold his black soul.
BRING HIM TO ME.
YOU WILL NOT DIE YET.
I WILL FIRST STRIP YOU OF EVERYTHING--AS YOU STRIPPED ME.
YOUR CROWN, YOUR BRIDE AND SON
YOUR DIGNITY AND YOUR FLESH.
AND THEN, IF I AM FEELING MERCIFUL...
I WILL KILL YOU.

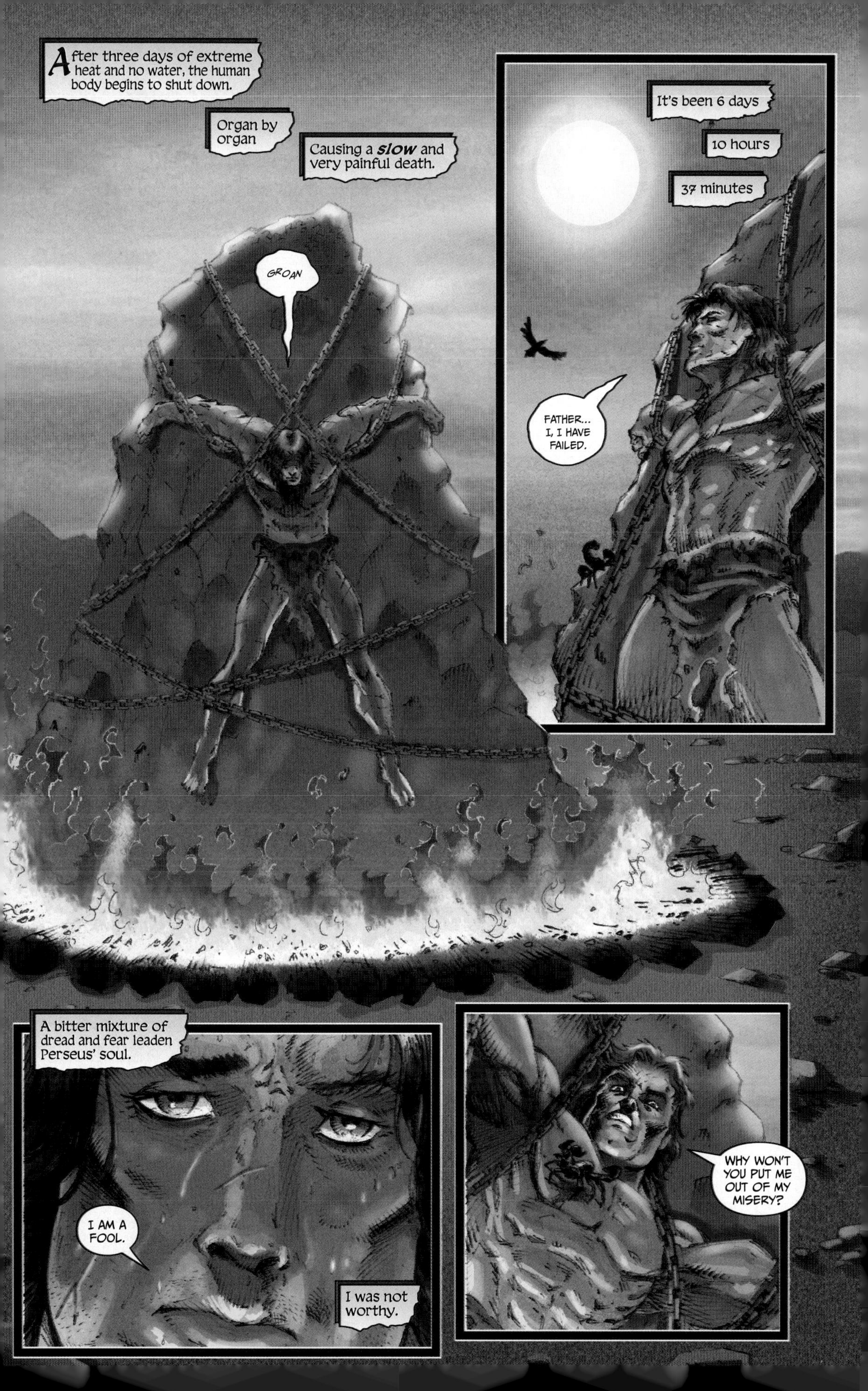
After three days of extreme heat and no water, the human body begins to shut down.
Organ by organ
Causing a *slow* and very painful death.
GROAN
It's been 6 days
10 hours
37 minutes
FATHER... I, I HAVE FAILED.
A bitter mixture of dread and fear leaden Perseus' soul.
I AM A FOOL.
I was not worthy.
WHY WON'T YOU PUT ME OUT OF MY MISERY?

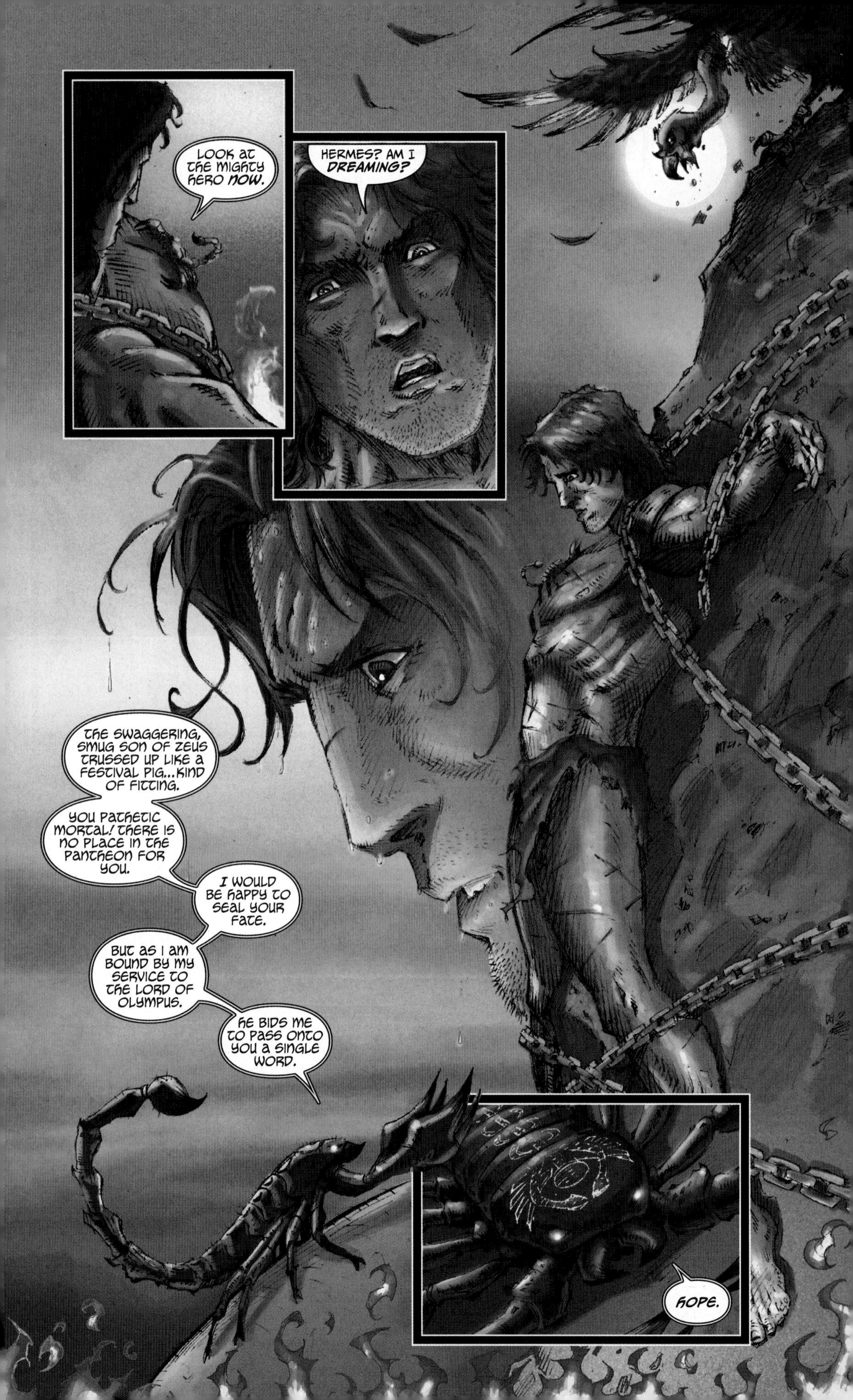
LOOK AT THE MIGHTY HERO NOW.
HERMES? AM I DREAMING?
THE SWAGGERING, SMUG SON OF ZEUS TRUSSED UP LIKE A FESTIVAL PIG...KIND OF FITTING.
YOU PATHETIC MORTAL! THERE IS NO PLACE IN THE PANTHEON FOR YOU.
I WOULD BE HAPPY TO SEAL YOUR FATE.
BUT AS I AM BOUND BY MY SERVICE TO THE LORD OF OLYMPUS.
HE BIDS ME TO PASS ONTO YOU A SINGLE WORD.
HOPE.

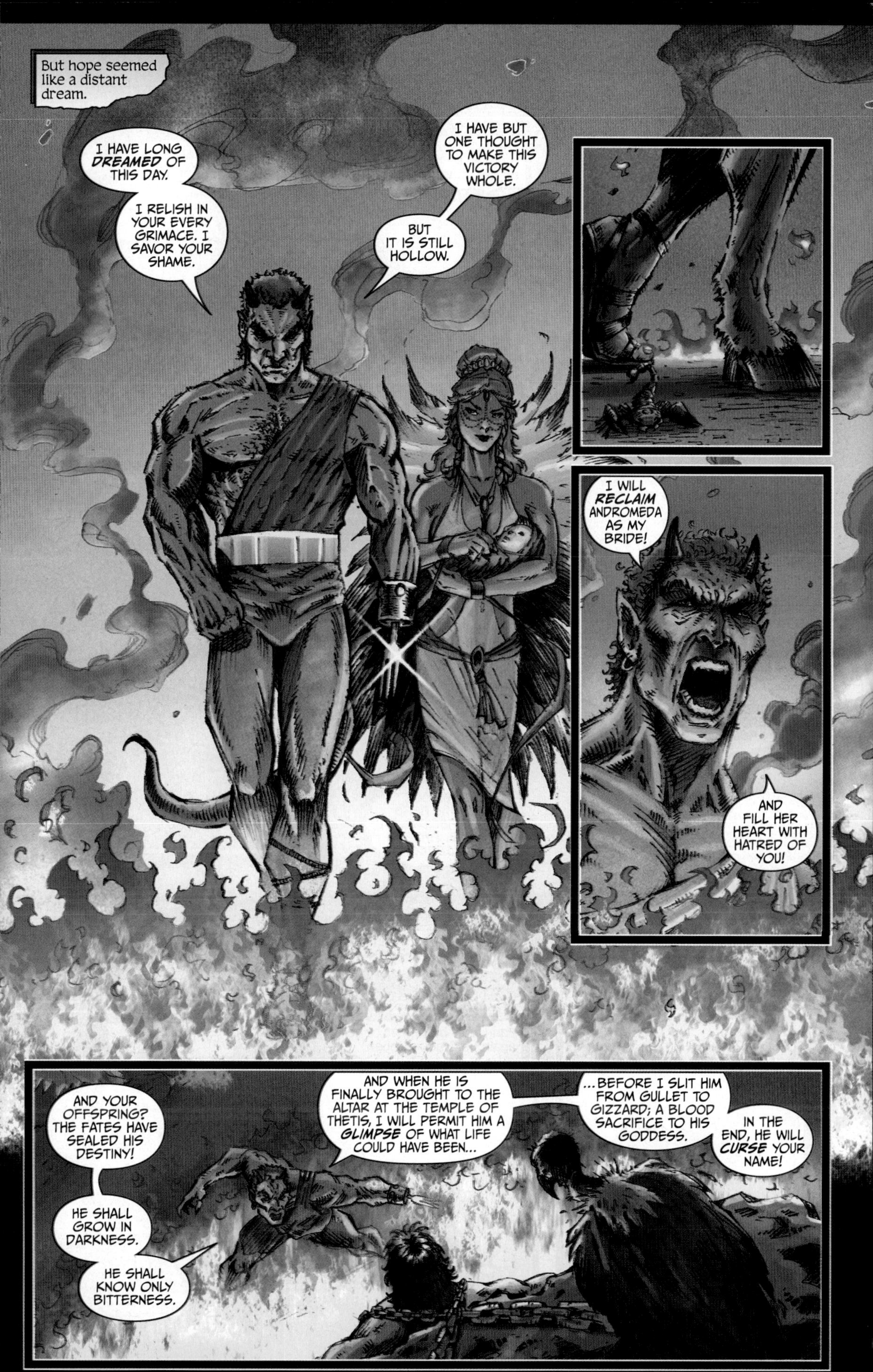
But hope seemed like a distant dream.
I HAVE LONG DREAMED OF THIS DAY.
I RELISH IN YOUR EVERY GRIMACE. I SAVOR YOUR SHAME.
I HAVE BUT ONE THOUGHT TO MAKE THIS VICTORY WHOLE.
BUT IT IS STILL HOLLOW.
I WILL RECLAIM ANDROMEDA AS MY BRIDE!
AND FILL HER HEART WITH HATRED OF YOU!
AND YOUR OFFSPRING? THE FATES HAVE SEALED HIS DESTINY!
HE SHALL GROW IN DARKNESS.
HE SHALL KNOW ONLY BITTERNESS.
AND WHEN HE IS FINALLY BROUGHT TO THE ALTAR AT THE TEMPLE OF THETIS, I WILL PERMIT HIM A GLIMPSE OF WHAT LIFE COULD HAVE BEEN...
...BEFORE I SLIT HIM FROM GULLET TO GIZZARD; A BLOOD SACRIFICE TO HIS GODDESS.
IN THE END, HE WILL CURSE YOUR NAME!

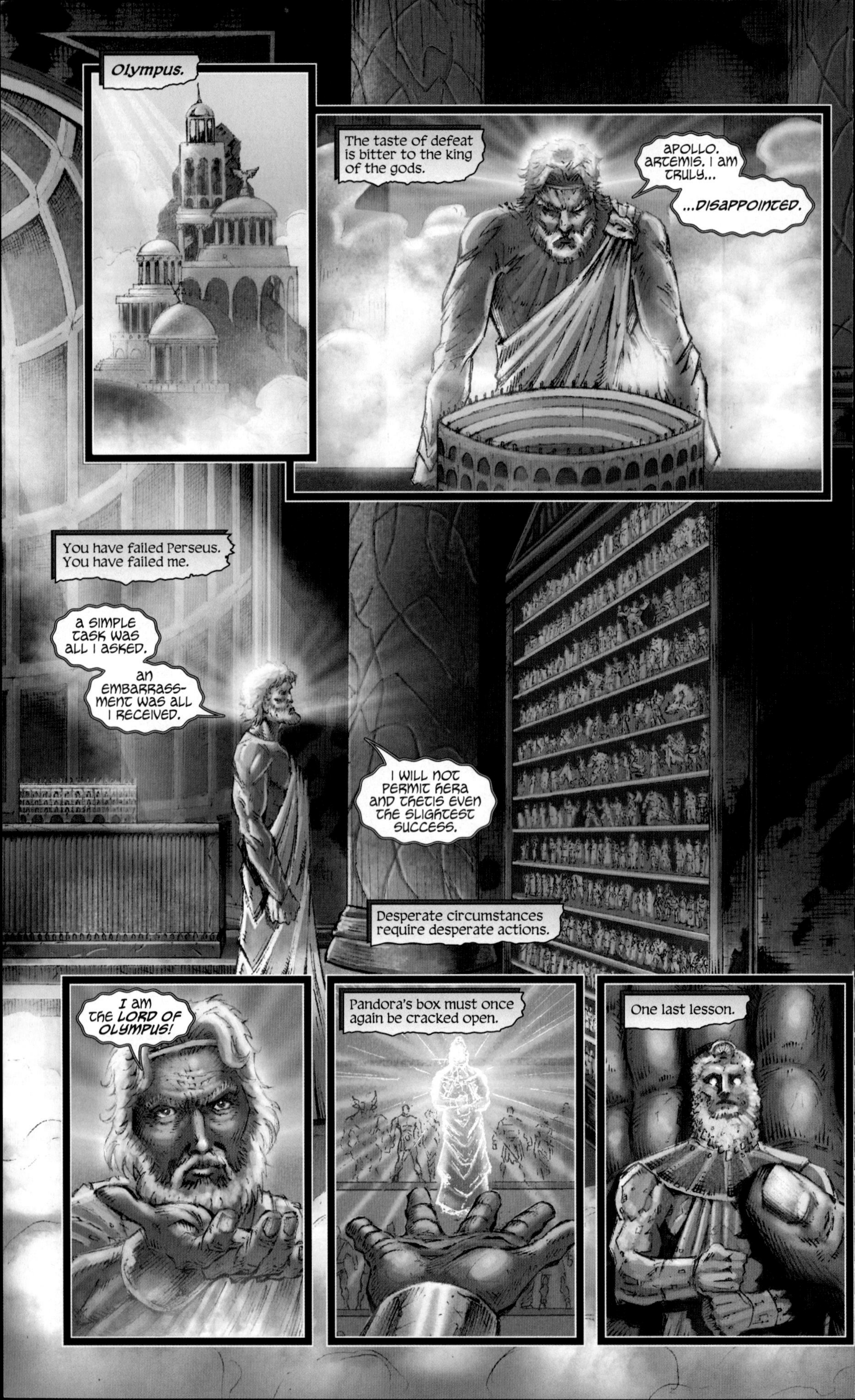

Olympus.
The taste of defeat is bitter to the king of the gods.
APOLLO. ARTEMIS. I AM TRULY...
...DISAPPOINTED.
You have failed Perseus. You have failed me.
A SIMPLE TASK WAS ALL I ASKED.
AN EMBARRASS-MENT WAS ALL I RECEIVED.
I WILL NOT PERMIT HERA AND THETIS EVEN THE SLIGHTEST SUCCESS.
Desperate circumstances require desperate actions.
I AM THE LORD OF OLYMPUS!
Pandora's box must once again be cracked open.
One last lesson.

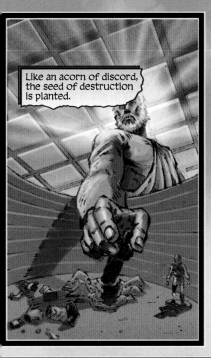

Like an acorn of discord, the seed of destruction is planted.

Ahh, MY CHILDREN, YOU SHOULD REMAIN IN TARTARUS FOR YOUR PITIFUL PERFORMANCE.

BUT I AM A MERCIFUL GOD.

YOU SUMMONED ME, FATHER?

DEAREST ATHENA. I CRAVE YOUR COUNSEL.

PERSEUS NEEDS A *NUDGE* IN THE RIGHT DIRECTION.

BUT TAKE HEED, DISCRETION IS OF THE *UTMOST* IMPORTANCE.

I HAVE THE PERFECT PLAN.

Though his heart be powered by gears and gizmos, Bubo unflaggingly proves to be a loyal and faithful *friend*.

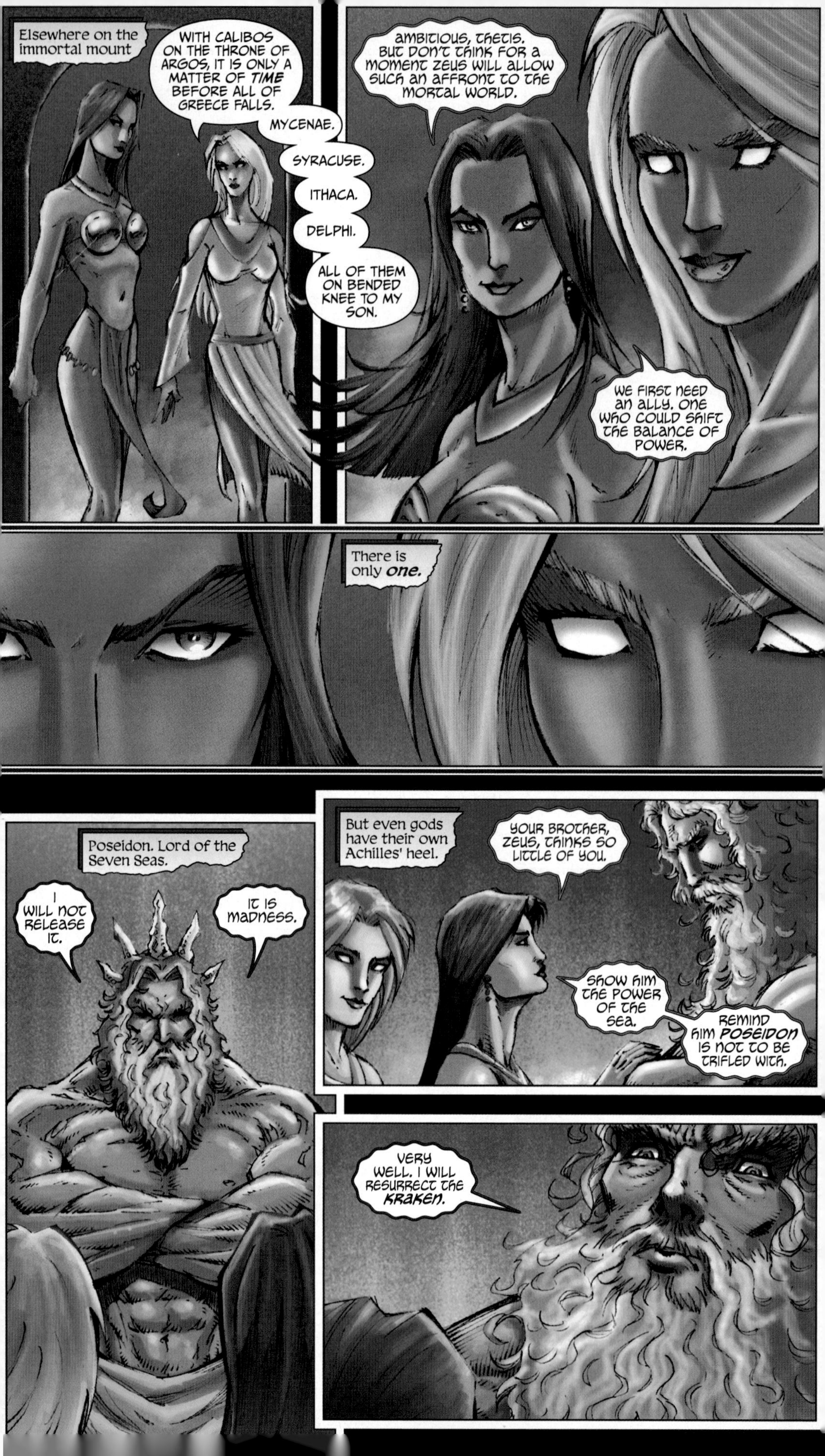

Elsewhere on the immortal mount
WITH CALIBOS ON THE THRONE OF ARGOS, IT IS ONLY A MATTER OF TIME BEFORE ALL OF GREECE FALLS.
MYCENAE.
SYRACUSE.
ITHACA.
DELPHI.
ALL OF THEM ON BENDED KNEE TO MY SON.
AMBITIOUS, THETIS. BUT DON'T THINK FOR A MOMENT ZEUS WILL ALLOW SUCH AN AFFRONT TO THE MORTAL WORLD.
WE FIRST NEED AN ALLY. ONE WHO COULD SHIFT THE BALANCE OF POWER.
There is only one.
Poseidon. Lord of the Seven Seas.
I WILL NOT RELEASE IT.
IT IS MADNESS.
But even gods have their own Achilles' heel.
YOUR BROTHER, ZEUS, THINKS SO LITTLE OF YOU.
SHOW HIM THE POWER OF THE SEA.
REMIND HIM POSEIDON IS NOT TO BE TRIFLED WITH.
VERY WELL. I WILL RESURRECT THE KRAKEN.

Long ago, the Titan Prometheus was condemned by the gods.

Each day vultures would rip out his inner organs.

Each night his body would be restored only to have the cycle begin again.

Century after century. Millennia after millennia.

Was this to be the fate of Perseus as well?

NHHZZZZZSCREEE

EEE

TIC TIIC

RRRAAHHHH!

WHHRRHOOHOO

As if possessed by the Furies...

TIC TIC

MY LITTLE SAVIOR.

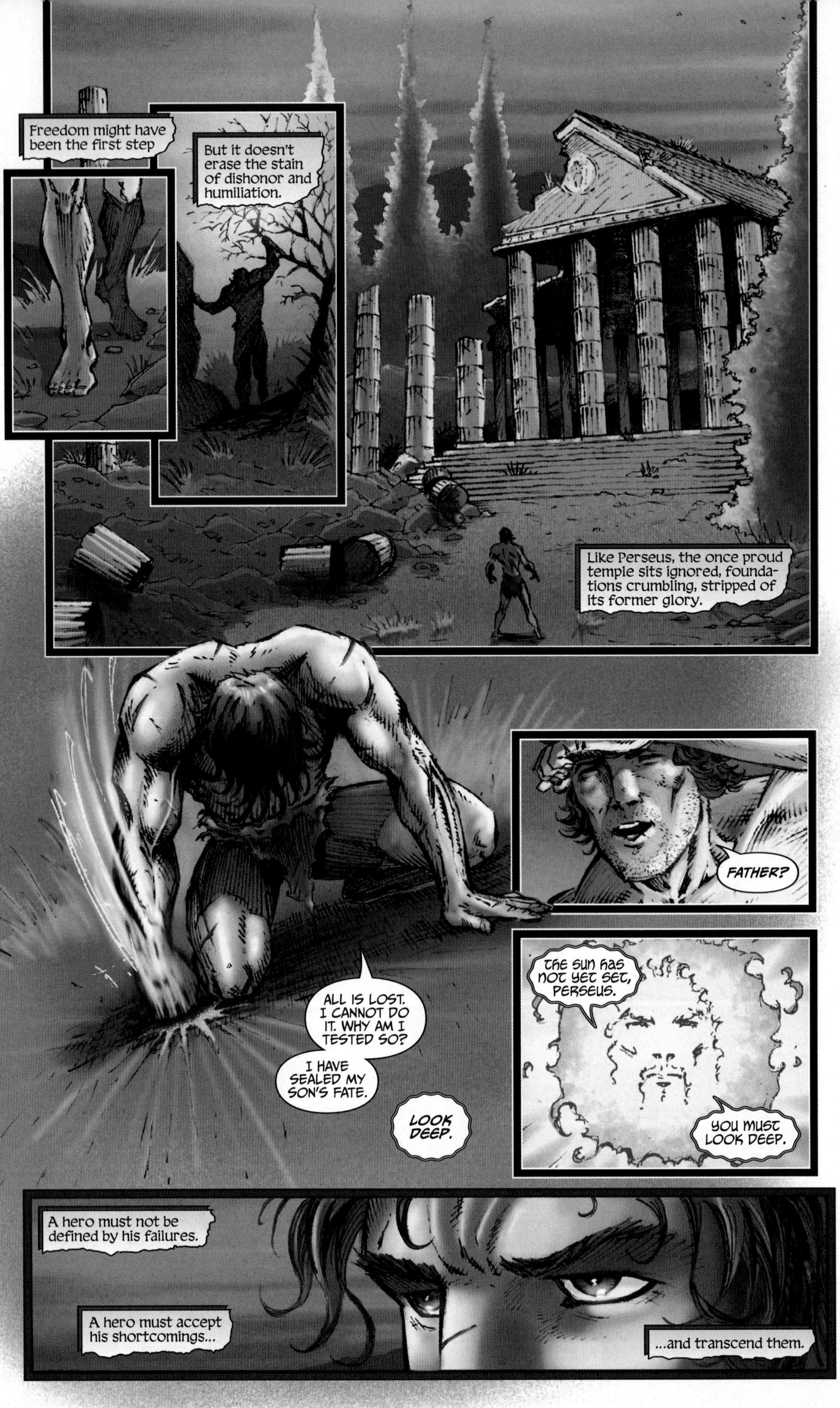
Freedom might have been the first step
But it doesn't erase the stain of dishonor and humiliation.
Like Perseus, the once proud temple sits ignored, foundations crumbling, stripped of its former glory.
FATHER?
ALL IS LOST. I CANNOT DO IT. WHY AM I TESTED SO?
I HAVE SEALED MY SON'S FATE.
THE SUN HAS NOT YET SET, PERSEUS.
YOU MUST LOOK DEEP.
LOOK DEEP.
A hero must not be defined by his failures.
A hero must accept his shortcomings...
...and transcend them.

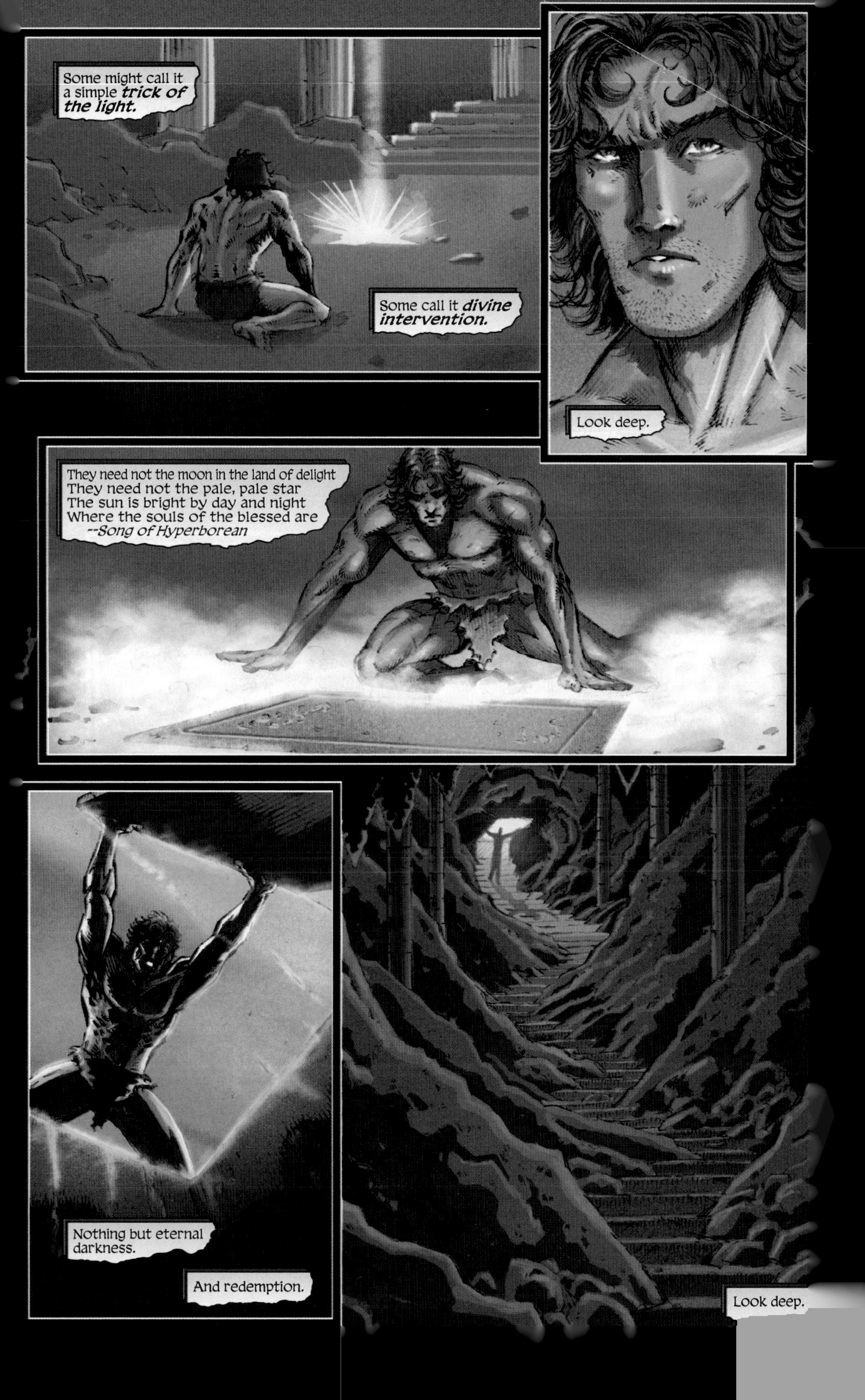
Some might call it a simple *trick of the light.*
Some call it *divine intervention.*
Look deep.
They need not the moon in the land of delight
They need not the pale, pale star
The sun is bright by day and night
Where the souls of the blessed are
--*Song of Hyperborean*
Nothing but eternal darkness.
And redemption.
Look deep.

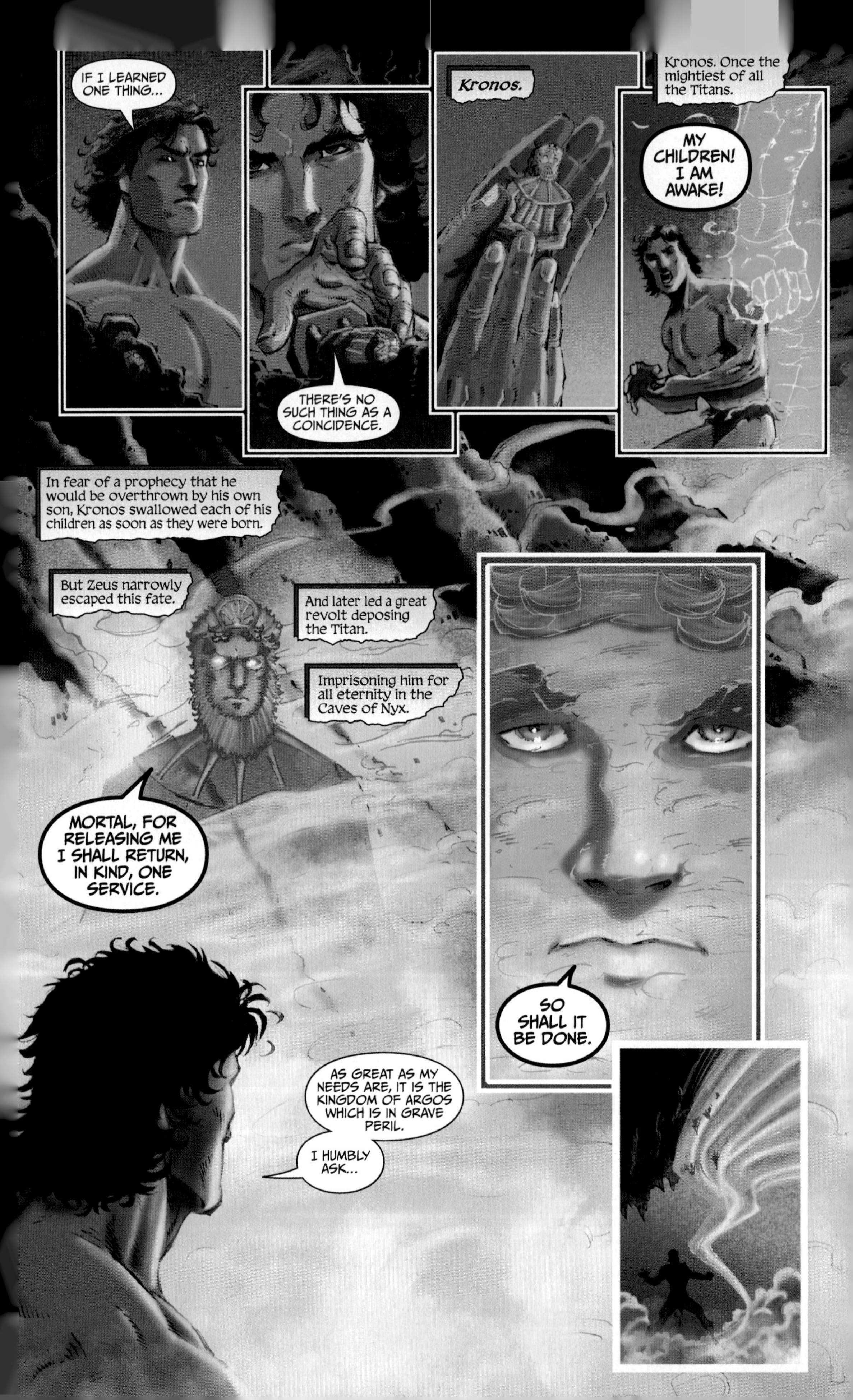
IF I LEARNED ONE THING...
THERE'S NO SUCH THING AS A COINCIDENCE.
Kronos.
Kronos. Once the mightiest of all the Titans.
MY CHILDREN! I AM AWAKE!
In fear of a prophecy that he would be overthrown by his own son, Kronos swallowed each of his children as soon as they were born.
But Zeus narrowly escaped this fate.
And later led a great revolt deposing the Titan.
Imprisoning him for all eternity in the Caves of Nyx.
MORTAL, FOR RELEASING ME I SHALL RETURN, IN KIND, ONE SERVICE.
AS GREAT AS MY NEEDS ARE, IT IS THE KINGDOM OF ARGOS WHICH IS IN GRAVE PERIL.
I HUMBLY ASK...
SO SHALL IT BE DONE.

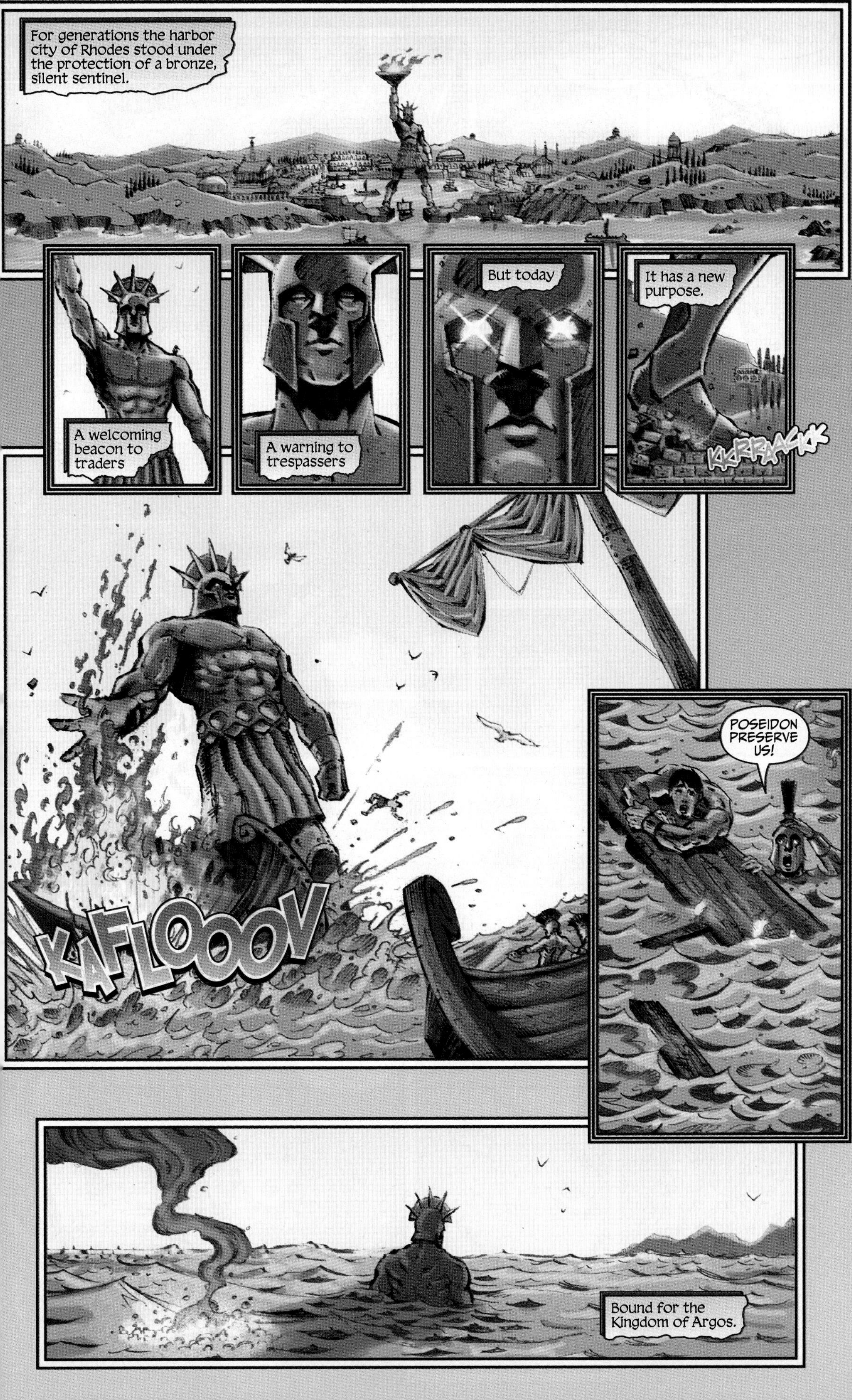
For generations the harbor city of Rhodes stood under the protection of a bronze, silent sentinel.
A welcoming beacon to traders
A warning to trespassers
But today
It has a new purpose.
KKRRAAKK
KAFLOOOV
POSEIDON PRESERVE US!
Bound for the Kingdom of Argos.

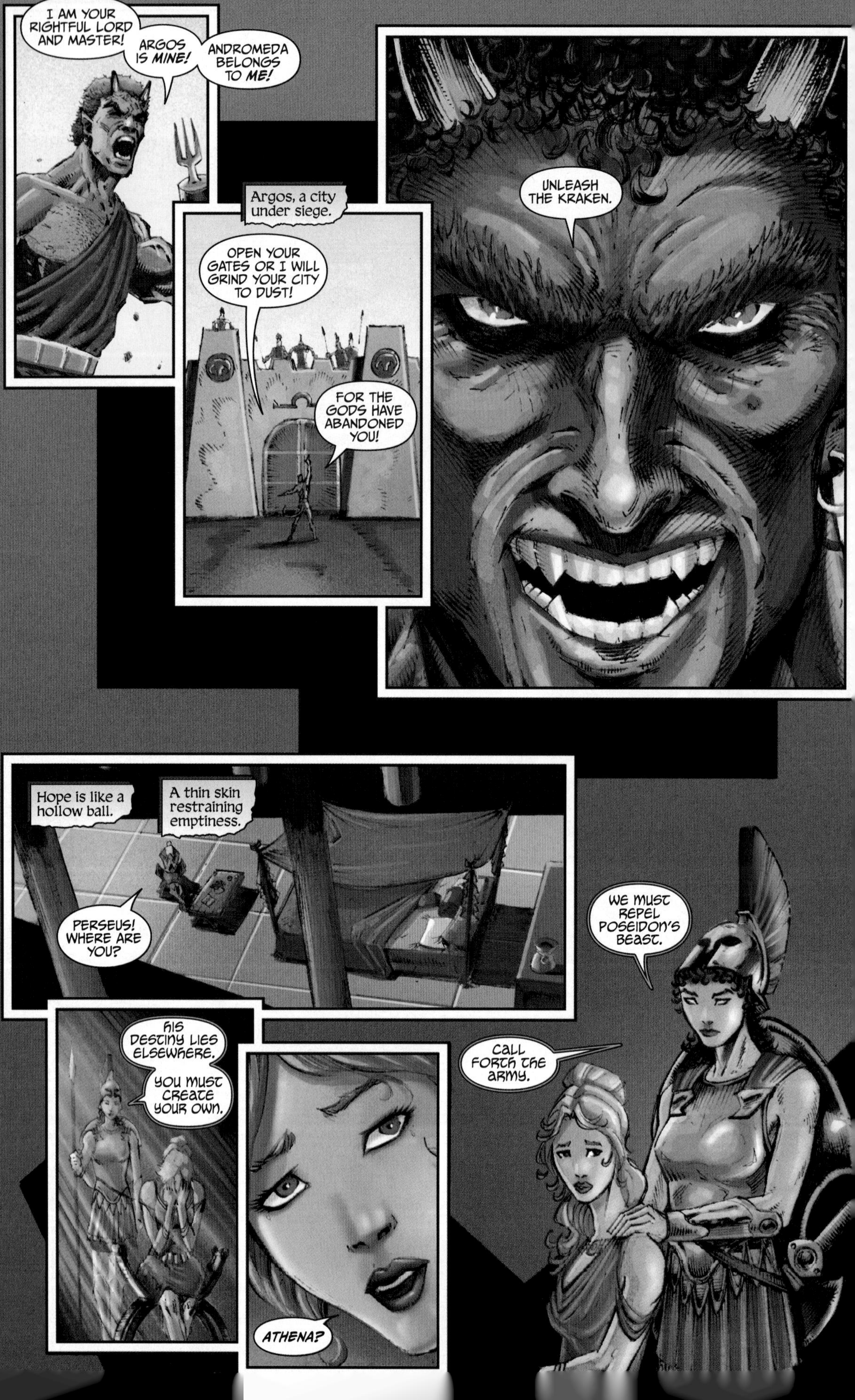
I AM YOUR RIGHTFUL LORD AND MASTER!
ARGOS IS MINE!
ANDROMEDA BELONGS TO ME!
Argos, a city under siege.
OPEN YOUR GATES OR I WILL GRIND YOUR CITY TO DUST!
FOR THE GODS HAVE ABANDONED YOU!
UNLEASH THE KRAKEN.
Hope is like a hollow ball.
A thin skin restraining emptiness.
PERSEUS! WHERE ARE YOU?
HIS DESTINY LIES ELSEWHERE.
YOU MUST CREATE YOUR OWN.
ATHENA?
WE MUST REPEL POSEIDON'S BEAST.
CALL FORTH THE ARMY.

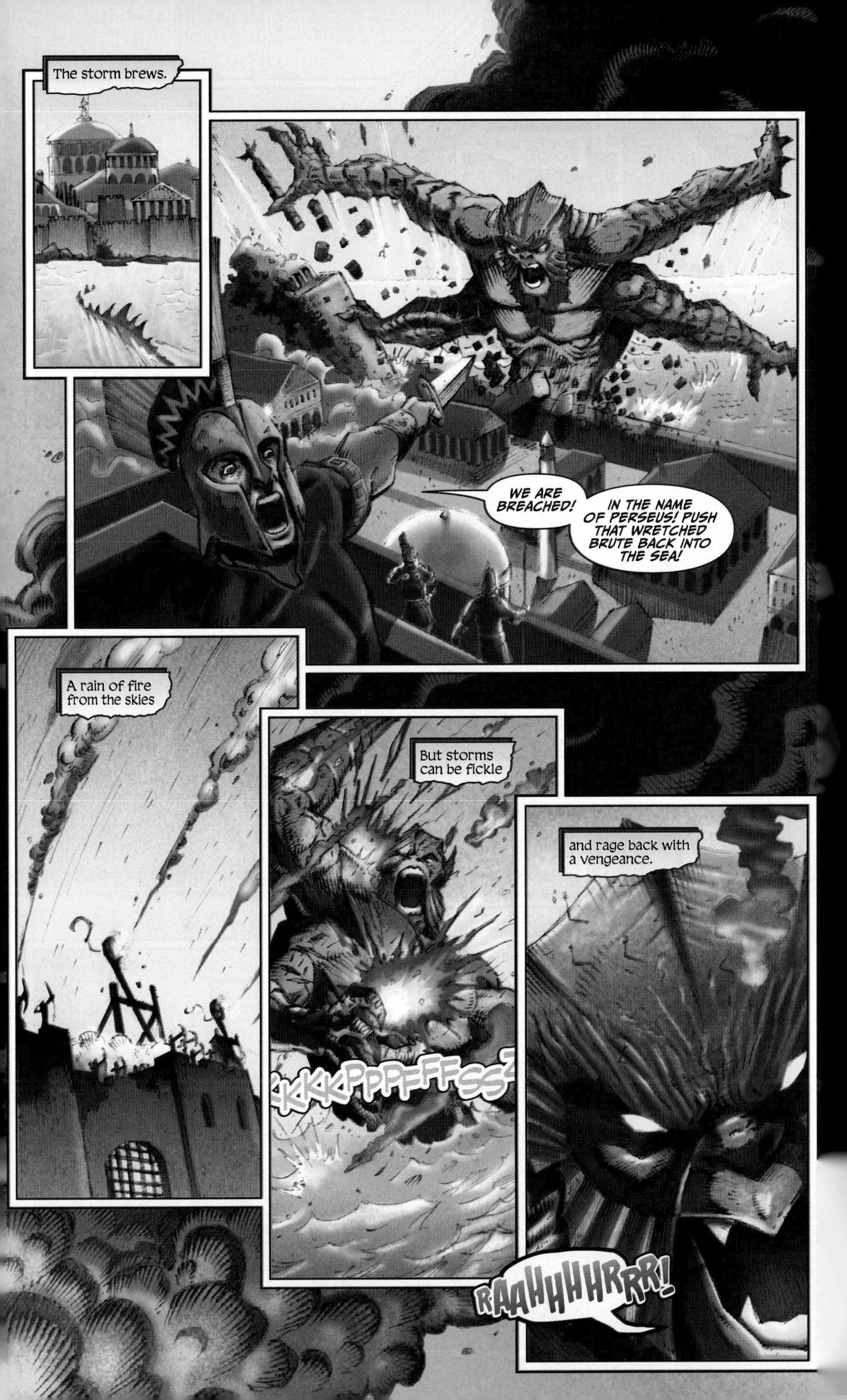
The storm brews.
WE ARE BREACHED!
IN THE NAME OF PERSEUS! PUSH THAT WRETCHED BRUTE BACK INTO THE SEA!
A rain of fire from the skies
But storms can be fickle
KKKKPPPFFFSS
and rage back with a vengeance.
RAAHHHHRRR!

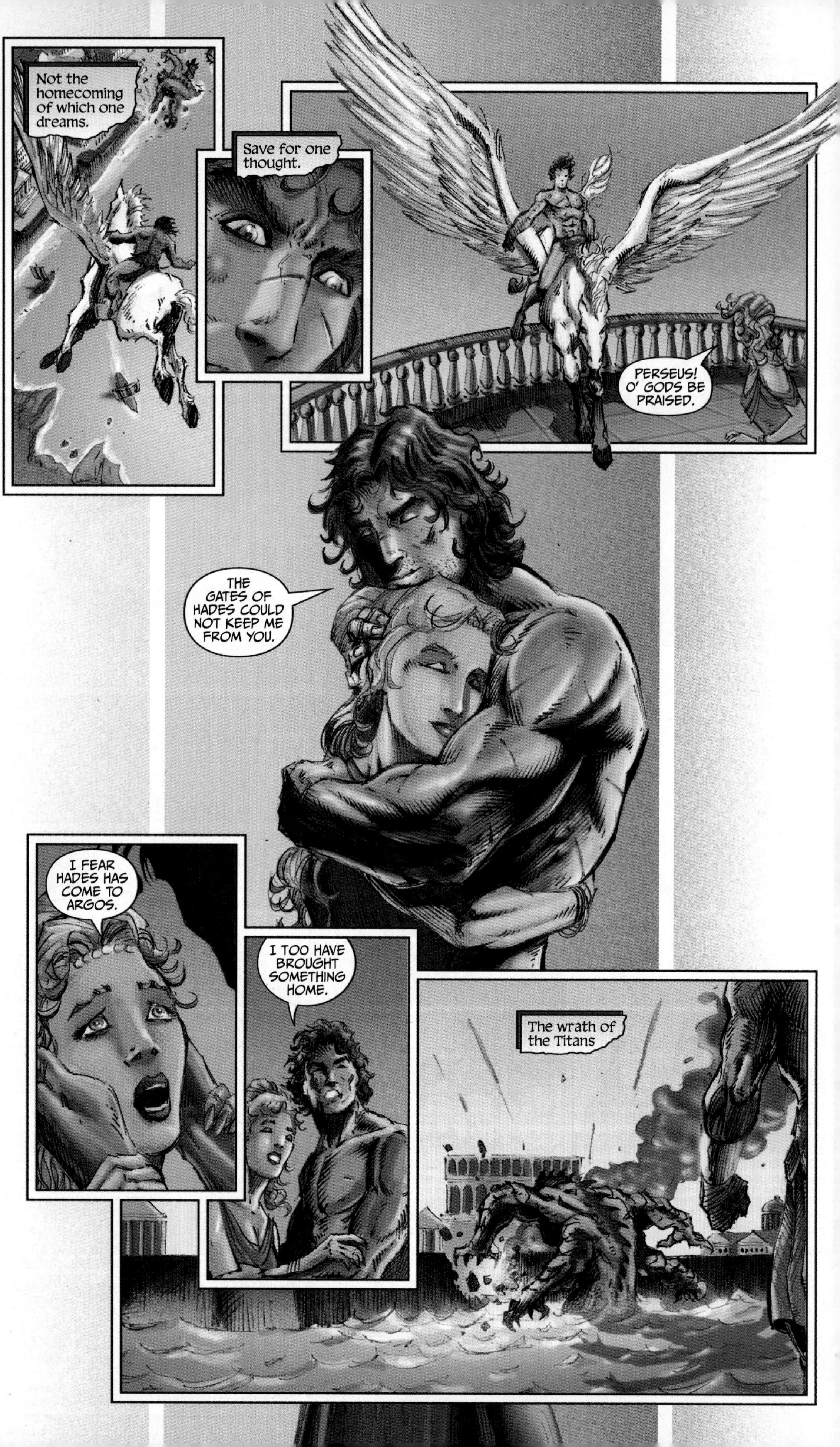
Not the homecoming of which one dreams.
Save for one thought.
PERSEUS! O' GODS BE PRAISED.
THE GATES OF HADES COULD NOT KEEP ME FROM YOU.
I FEAR HADES HAS COME TO ARGOS.
I TOO HAVE BROUGHT SOMETHING HOME.
The wrath of the Titans

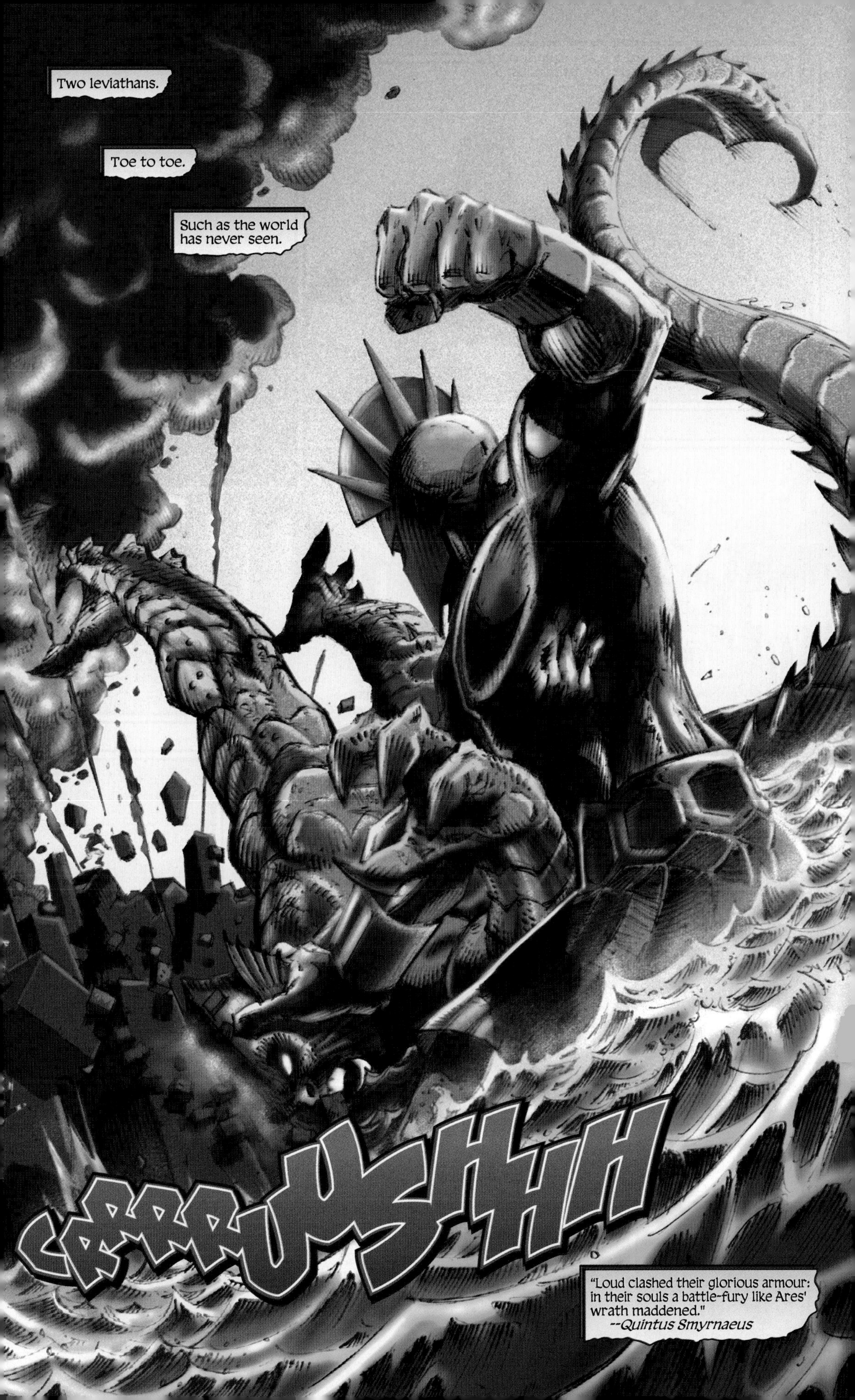
Two leviathans.
Toe to toe.
Such as the world has never seen.
CRRRUUSHHH
"Loud clashed their glorious armour: in their souls a battle-fury like Ares' wrath maddened."
--Quintus Smyrnaeus

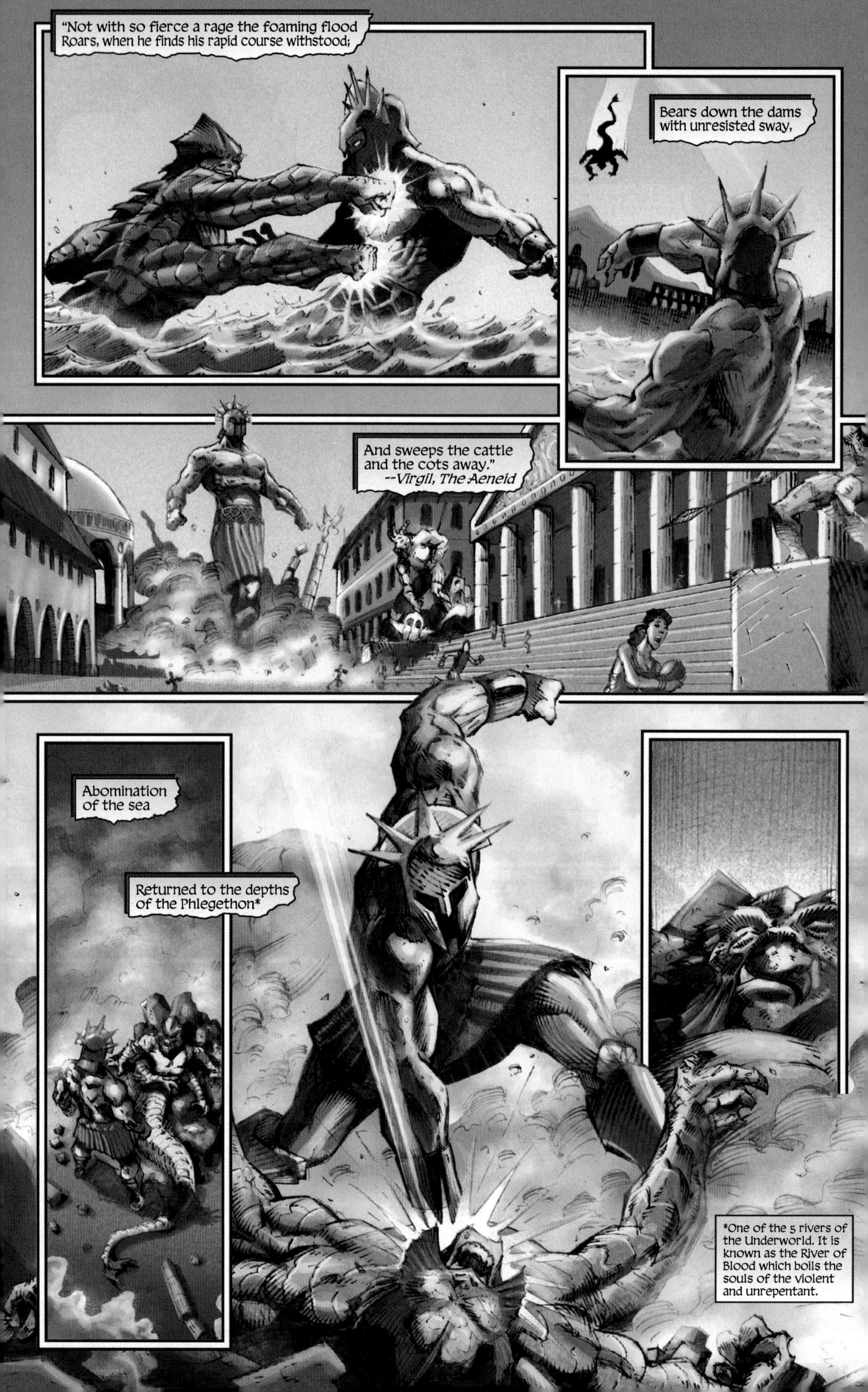
"Not with so fierce a rage the foaming flood
Roars, when he finds his rapid course withstood;
Bears down the dams
with unresisted sway,
And sweeps the cattle
and the cots away."
--Virgil, The Aeneid
Abomination
of the sea
Returned to the depths
of the Phlegethon*
*One of the 5 rivers of
the Underworld. It is
known as the River of
Blood which boils the
souls of the violent
and unrepentant.

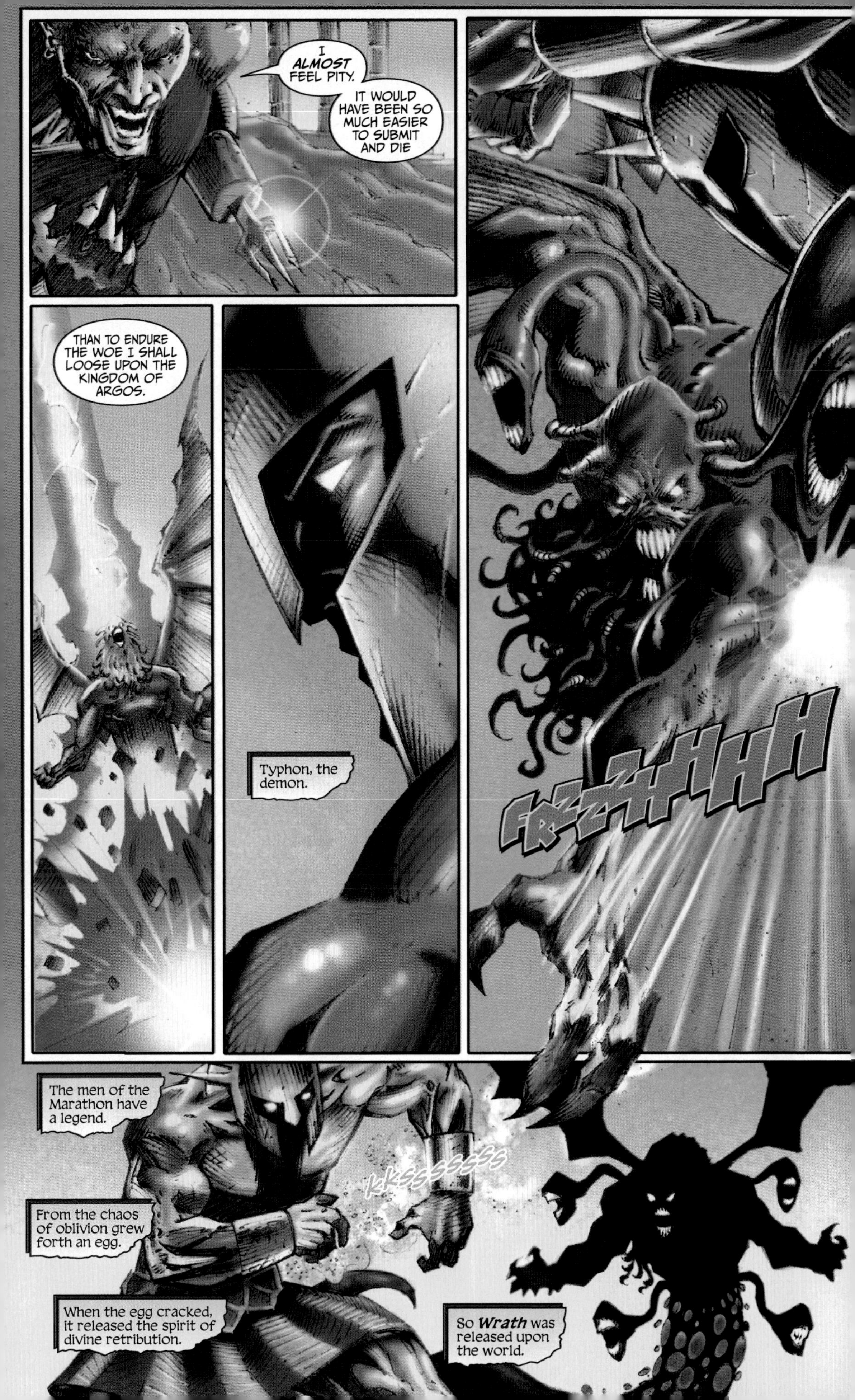
I ALMOST FEEL PITY.
IT WOULD HAVE BEEN SO MUCH EASIER TO SUBMIT AND DIE
THAN TO ENDURE THE WOE I SHALL LOOSE UPON THE KINGDOM OF ARGOS.
Typhon, the demon.
FRZZHHHH
The men of the Marathon have a legend.
KKSSSSSSSS
From the chaos of oblivion grew forth an egg.
When the egg cracked, it released the spirit of divine retribution.
So Wrath was released upon the world.

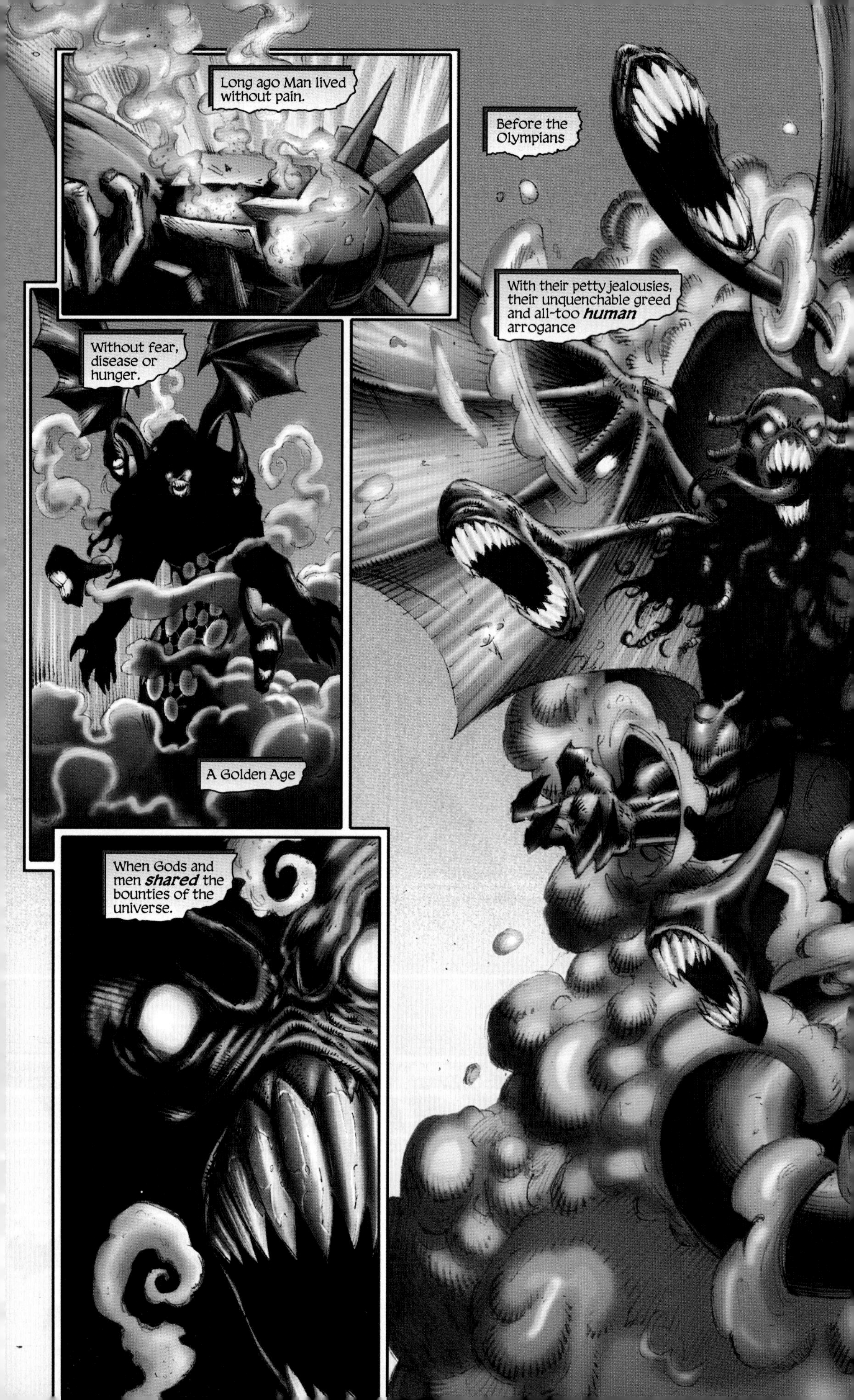

Long ago Man lived without pain.
Without fear, disease or hunger.
A Golden Age
When Gods and men *shared* the bounties of the universe.
Before the Olympians
With their petty jealousies, their unquenchable greed and all-too ***human*** arrogance

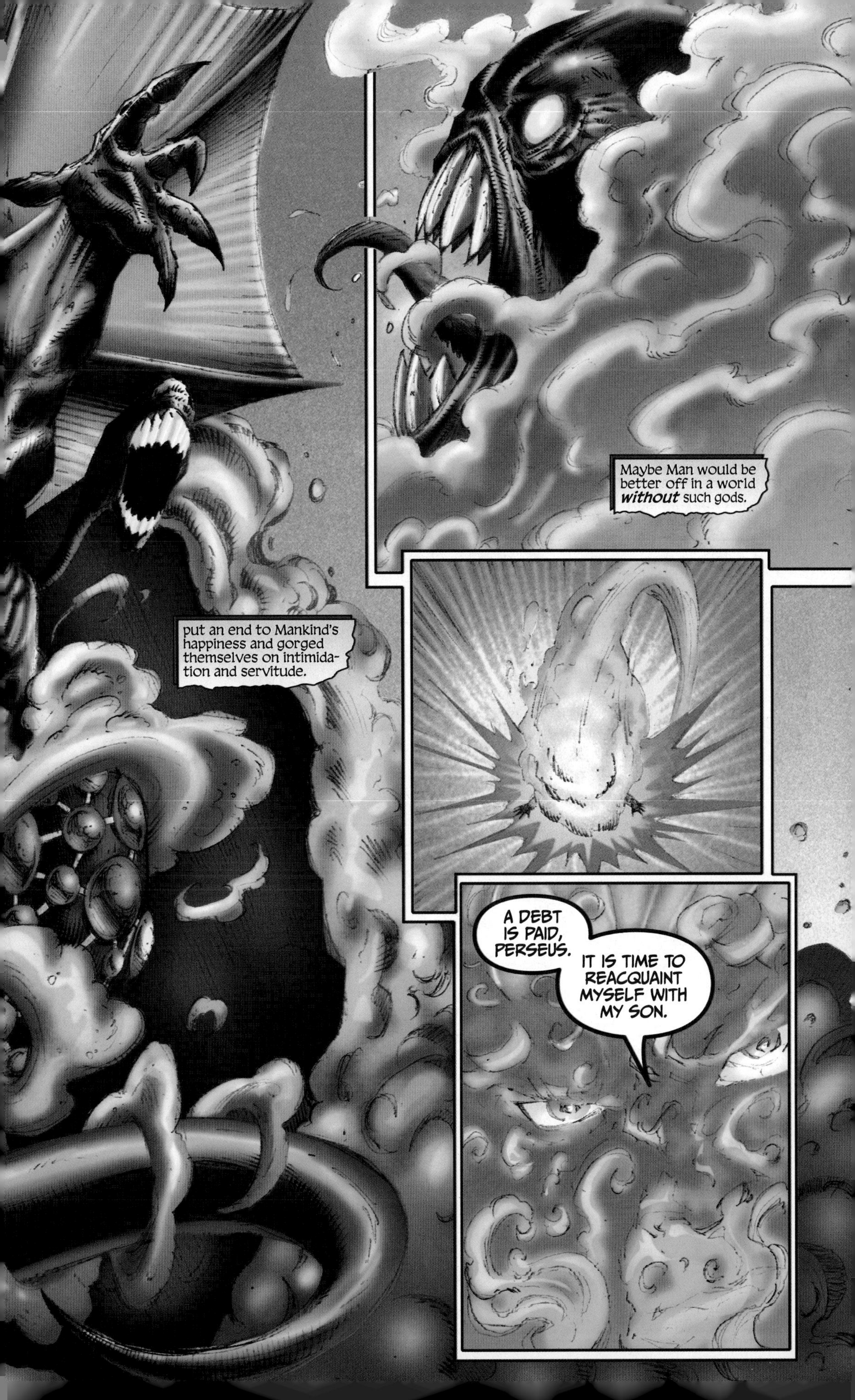
Maybe Man would be better off in a world ***without*** such gods.
put an end to Mankind's happiness and gorged themselves on intimidation and servitude.
A DEBT IS PAID, PERSEUS.
IT IS TIME TO REACQUAINT MYSELF WITH MY SON.

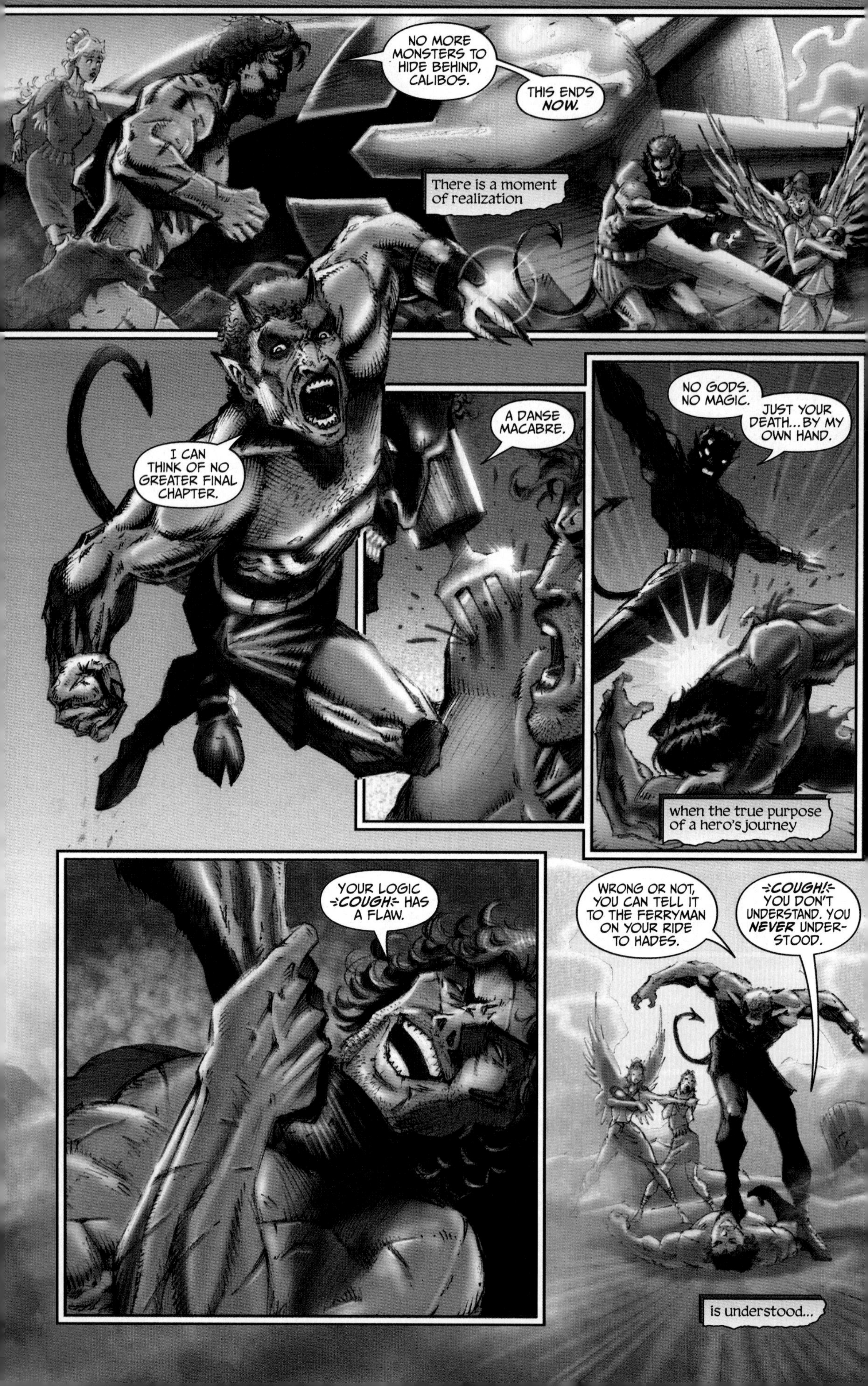
NO MORE MONSTERS TO HIDE BEHIND, CALIBOS.
THIS ENDS NOW.
There is a moment of realization
I CAN THINK OF NO GREATER FINAL CHAPTER.
A DANSE MACABRE.
NO GODS. NO MAGIC.
JUST YOUR DEATH...BY MY OWN HAND.
when the true purpose of a hero's journey
YOUR LOGIC -COUGH- HAS A FLAW.
WRONG OR NOT, YOU CAN TELL IT TO THE FERRYMAN ON YOUR RIDE TO HADES.
-COUGH!- YOU DON'T UNDERSTAND. YOU NEVER UNDERSTOOD.
is understood...

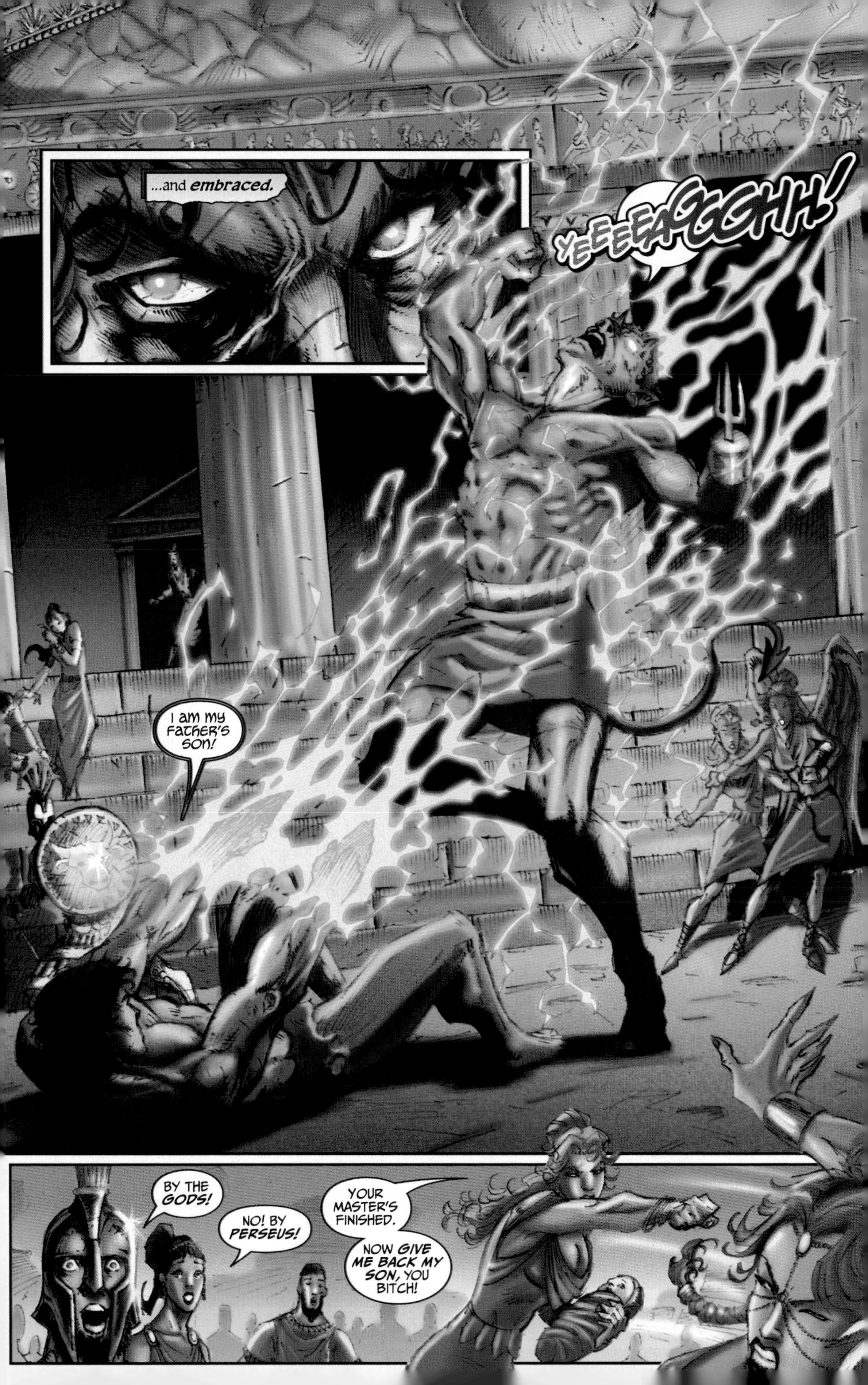
...and embraced.
YEEEEAGGGHH!
I am my father's son!
BY THE GODS!
NO! BY PERSEUS!
YOUR MASTER'S FINISHED.
NOW GIVE ME BACK MY SON, YOU BITCH!

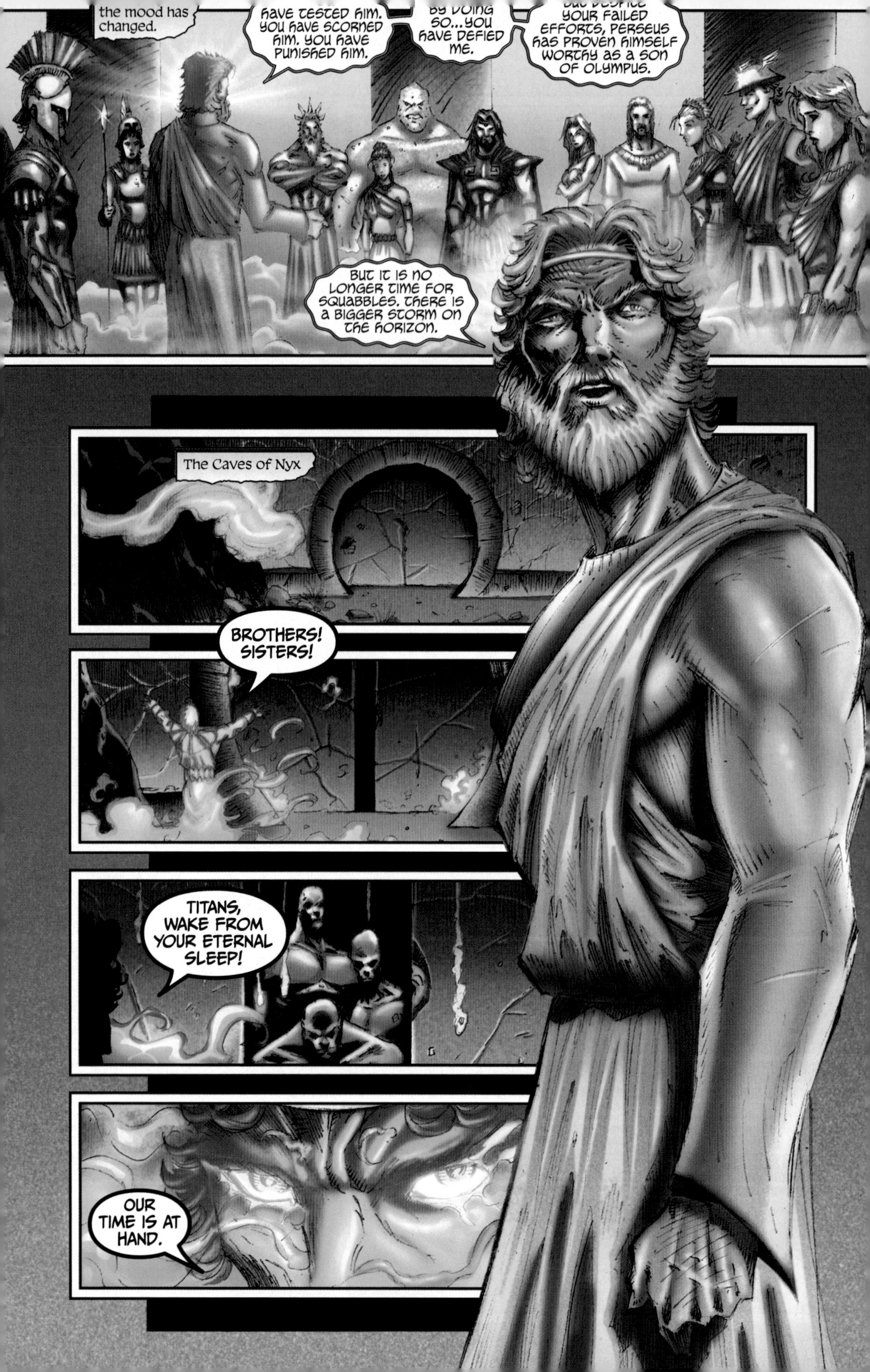
the mood has changed.
have tested him. You have scorned him. You have punished him.
so...you have defied me.
your failed efforts, Perseus has proven himself worthy as a son of Olympus.
But it is no longer time for squabbles. There is a bigger storm on the horizon.
The Caves of Nyx
BROTHERS! SISTERS!
TITANS, WAKE FROM YOUR ETERNAL SLEEP!
OUR TIME IS AT HAND.

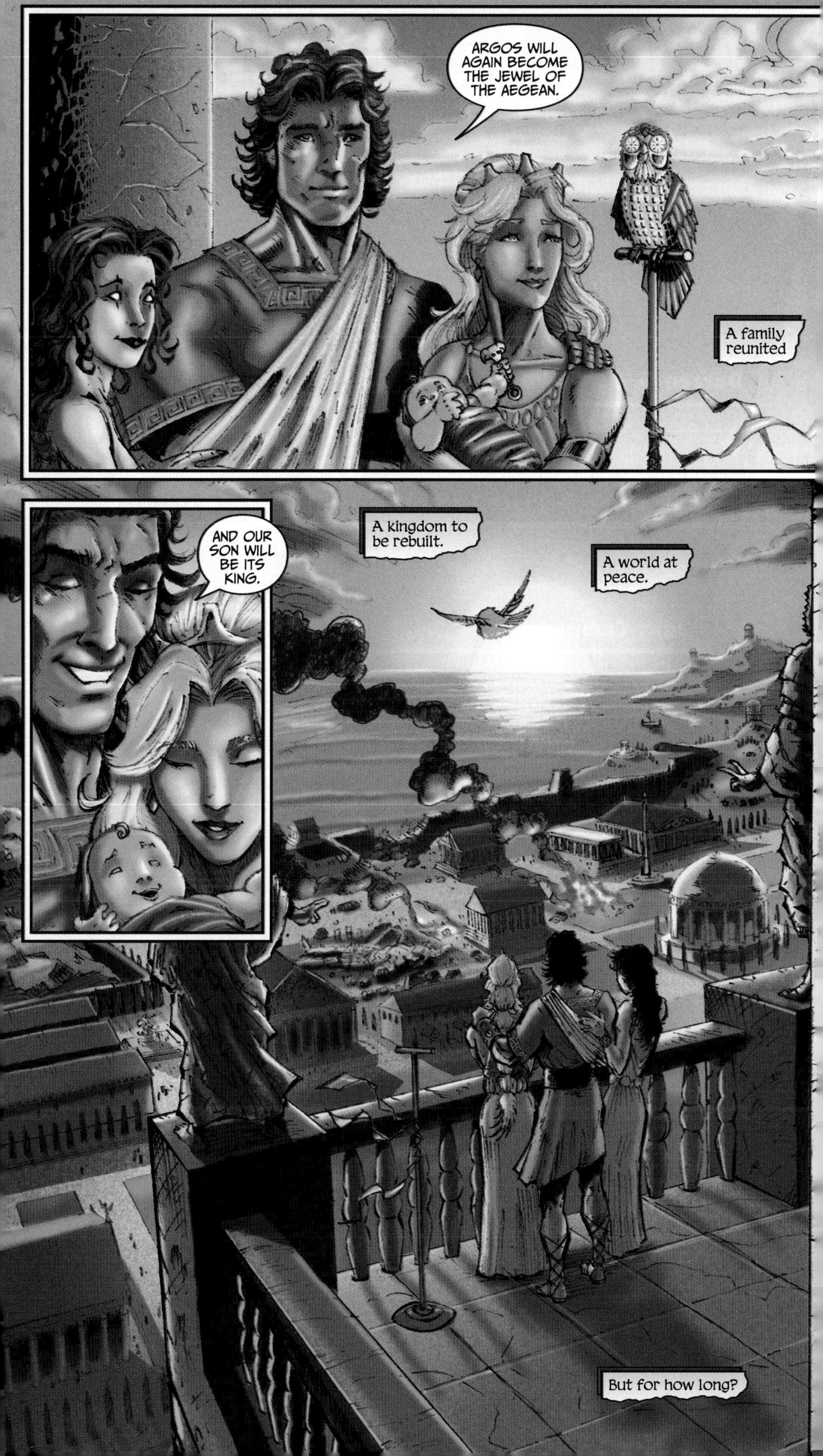
ARGOS WILL AGAIN BECOME THE JEWEL OF THE AEGEAN.
A family reunited
AND OUR SON WILL BE ITS KING.
A kingdom to be rebuilt.
A world at peace.
But for how long?

BLUEWATER COMICS

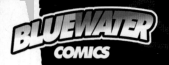

Ray Harryhausen Presents

WRATH OF THE TITANS

Cover by: Nadir Balan

Darren G. Davis & Scott Davis — Writers

Nadir Balan & Jason Metcalf — Pencilers

Joey Campos — Colorist

Chris Studabaker — Letterer

Darren G. Davis — Graphics

Darren G. Davis
Publisher

Jason Schultz
Vice President

Lisa K. Brause
Entertainment Manager

Ryan Scott Ottney
Communications Coordinator

Patrick Foster
Logo Design

Chris Studabaker
Production

BLUEWATER COMICS

Special Thanks to
Ray Harryhausen
&
Arnold Kunert

www.bluewaterprod.com